T0040265

starting
YOUR
CAREER as a
MUSICIAN

NEIL TORTORELLA

ALLWORTH PRESS
NEW YORK

Allworth Press books may be purchased in bulk at special discounts for sales promotion, corporate gifts, fund-raising, or educational purposes. Special editions can also be created to specifications. For details, contact the Special Sales Department, Allworth Press, 307 West 36th Street, 11th Floor, New York, NY 10018 or info@skyhorsepublishing.com.

15 14 13 12 11 5 4 3 2 1

Published by Allworth Press,
an imprint of Skyhorse Publishing, Inc.
307 West 36th Street, 11th Floor, New York, NY 10018.

Allworth Press® is a registered trademark of Skyhorse Publishing, Inc.®, a Delaware corporation.

www.allworth.com

Cover design by Mary Belibasakis

Library of Congress Cataloging-in-Publication Data is available on file.

ISBN: 978-1-58115-928-8

Printed in the United States of America

These pages are dedicated to my son, Alex, who is the light of my life, one of the best guitar players I know, and a brilliant all-around musician. They are also dedicated to my early band mates, Jonathan "Sam" Wuhrer, Carmine Pinto, Tom Brigante, and Phil Perne. These guys are some of the best musicians I know, and they taught me so much along our wildly weird way. And, of course, to all my readers and struggling musicians: My hope is that the words within aid you on your musical journey.

Contents

Introduction

M usic: It's a powerful thing. Music paints a sonic picture that can make us laugh or cry. A song can bring back the memory of a moment in time or transport us to another place. Voltaire is credited with saying, "With great power comes great responsibility." And so it is for the musician.

When musicians wield their instruments, they have a responsibility to their audience. That audience might be a sold-out stadium crowd or simply the musician sitting alone, playing to express what's in his or her heart. Either way, it's an emotional experience—at least it should be. There are expressive musicians, and there are mechanics. Mechanics may know the notes and tempo, but there's no feeling or emotion in their efforts.

A musician's instrument should be an extension of himself or herself. Where the instrument ends and the artist begins should be transparent. Great players are ones who know their instruments so well, they don't need to think about the instruments. The passion within is automatically passed through to the instrument.

Music is a universal language. It's hardwired within us. A song played in Kansas or Outer Mongolia will usually evoke the same emotional response. There's a load of research that's been done on the psycho- logical effects of music on human emotion. But I believe that when all is said and done, the good or great musician understands this language intuitively. Sure, the mechanical musician can play a song, but without an understanding of the nuances of the language, the song is just a collection of notes and some musical notation on a piece of paper. It will always lack those elusive elements of heart and soul.

A CAREER IN MUSIC

With these definitions in place, it's time to start talking, or rather writing, about a career in music. At the top of the list is the fact that it's not easy. A search on YouTube will quickly demonstrate that there's no shortage of talent out there. If you expect to have a musical career, talent should be a given.

Even if you're the best player on the planet, it doesn't matter much if nobody hears you. That means it is critical to aggressively promote yourself or your band. Right about now, you're likely thinking, "But I'll be selling out." Don't sweat it. You're not. If you truly believe you have something of value to offer an audience, you're doing people a favor by telling them about you and your music. If you don't promote, you'll probably find yourself sitting on your sofa playing gut-wrenching songs of love gone wrong to an audience of one—yourself—while thinking, "Why can't I get any gigs?"

Beyond promotion, becoming a successful musician means setting goals; understanding your audience; having some basic business skills; learning and growing as an artist; and, most important, having drive and the right, positive attitude. The good news is that all these things can be learned. It just takes the willingness to learn them and put your knowledge into action.

Unless you happen to be clairvoyant, you don't know what the future holds. Lao Tzu is credited with saying, "The journey of one thousand miles begins with a single step." So, you've got to start somewhere. Hopefully this book will help you take that first step and then move forward. Who knows? You might just become the next big sensation—or not. You might get a steady stream of weekend club gigs, find a job as the music minister at a church, or teach. It all depends on your goals.

THE STATE OF THE MUSIC INDUSTRY

There's more good news. Well, more of a double-edged sword type of news. There has never been a better time to be a musician, whether you're a solo act or with a band, because of the technology available to artists. On the flip side, there's significantly more competition, all of whom are vying for fame and fortune, the gig at the bar down the street, or that minister of music job that just opened up.

A bit of a history lesson is in order. In 1877, Thomas Edison, while tinkering with a new telegraph gizmo, noticed speech-like noises emanating from the device. He toyed with it a bit more and developed the first phonograph. He recorded "Mary Had A Little Lamb" by the end of 1877. The song became an instant, chart-topping hit, mostly because it was the only successful recording of a human voice in existence. And so the recording industry was born.

Edison's phonograph evolved into the gramophone, the graphophone, the Victrola, and, eventually, eight-track and cassette tapes followed by compact discs (CDs). Music was now widely available to the population. Plus, it was relatively easy to obtain; all it took was a trip to the record or department store. Some folks opted for the convenience of joining record clubs and received their melodic orders via the Postal Service.

Then came the beginning of the death throes for the record labels. The Grim Reaper came in the form of digital music, the Internet, file sharing, and various other threats to an industry that had become bloated and huge.

The label, also known as the record company, is responsible for producing, promoting, marketing, distributing, and selling an album. The label sinks a load of dough into an artist, betting the audience will love the performer. If the people in the audience do, they buy CDs, tickets to concerts, and various merchandise. In return, the label takes the lion's share of the profit.

In the past, an artist or band had little hope of making it big without being discovered by an A&R person working for a label. (*A&R* stands for "artists and repertoire"; in some circles, mostly musicians', it stands for "attitude and rejection.") A&R people are powerful in the record industry. They scout talent and sign the winners. They also nurture the band, aid in song selection, find the right producer, and act as the liaison between all the various departments within the record company, among other tasks.

When an artist is signed, the full fury of the label is unleashed. Marketing plans are developed, public relations efforts are launched, distribution channels are arranged, and radio and other broadcast media are wooed. Then there are the more mundane tasks involving legal issues, bookkeeping, and finances. And, of course, there are the tour booking arrangements made either through an in-house department or by contract with an outside booking agent or agency.

The point here is that all of this takes money—lots and lots of money. After everybody takes a piece of the revenue pie, unless the artist becomes a platinum superstar, he or she is often left with a royalty that might be just enough to buy a burger and, perhaps, some fries.

All this worked fine for years—at least it worked fine for the record companies. As for the artists . . . well . . . it didn't always work out so great for some of them. But that's another story.

Bloated and huge things tend to move slowly. Therein lies the problem with monolithic record companies. With the advent of the digital age, the Internet, mp3s, and the like, things started moving at the speed of light. The labels simply couldn't keep up. They were complacent and set in their ways. Add to the mix plummeting CD sales, file sharing sites, and blatant musical piracy, and the recording industry began to look something like the portrait of Dorian Grey. Strikingly handsome and youthful on the surface, but decaying just below.

Then, along came Apple's iTunes, which focuses largely on selling singles. Record companies typically make money on album sales. Although sites such as Napster pre-dated iTunes, the latter, when paired with the iPod, essentially changed the distribution model for music sales. With almost 80 percent of the legal digital music market, iTunes became the top dog in the digital music arena. The record companies, albeit reluctantly, had no choice but to dance with iTunes because that's where people were buying. People like instant gratification, and Apple gave it to them. This is a feat that the traditional record company model simply couldn't accomplish. Other threats included Internet-based radio services such as Spotify and Pandora.

As if iTunes, Spotify, Pandora, and other services didn't leave enough of a gaping wound, piracy was a strike to the heart. Piracy is, for all intents and purposes, stealing. Yet, while most people wouldn't think of going into a store and getting a five-finger discount on a product, they think nothing of sharing tunes illegally. This might entail emailing a friend a cool new song, downloading mp3s from a site without paying for them, or burning a CD of an album to pass along to someone else. Sure, it seems innocent enough, but it costs the record companies millions or more in lost revenue—and that's not to mention the loss of revenue for the artists. These are the people who created the music and make their living from it.

To battle this, record companies are struggling to find new revenue streams. The 360 deal, also known as a multiple rights deal, is becoming popular, especially with larger record companies. This arrangement allows the record company to receive a percentage of *all* of a band's or individual artist's earnings. That means concert ticket sales, merchandise, endorsements, and so forth—everything. In return, the label agrees to promote the artist for a longer period of time and work to develop new opportunities for the artist. Some labels are seeking to exploit, or further exploit, licensing deals. But, any way you cut it, the traditional label model is in deep trouble.

WHAT DOES THIS MEAN FOR THE MUSICIAN?

Ironically, the doom and gloom hovering around the record companies spells opportunity for the smart and savvy musician. Rather than being at the mercy of a faceless corporation, questionable A&R executives, bad contracts, and paltry royalties, artists are taking control of their work and the direction of their careers.

Artists now have the ability to open a one-on-one dialogue with their fans via social media and various online tools. They can learn what their fans like and want. That's pretty valuable information and sure beats guessing.

Collaboration tools online abound. Artists no longer need to work in a vacuum. These tools, such as SoundCloud and Indaba, allow musicians and even fans to share thoughts and ideas, tracks, and more.

Many bands are bypassing the record companies altogether, opting to promote directly to their fans. In the past, this would have been an impossible undertaking. Twenty-first century technology changed that. Bands and solo artists are, more and more, becoming authentic small businesses whose products are music, live performances, merchandise, and more. Online tools, such as Topspin, ReverbNation, and FanBridge, are constantly being developed or improved to help them do it.

Is it easy? No. Profitable? Perhaps. When a band decides to go it alone, it means that in addition to rehearsing, performing, writing, and all the other usual musical tasks, the band members also need to handle all the tasks normally done by the record company. Those include tasks such as marketing, public relations, networking, schmoozing the media, keeping an eye on the books, and managing the financial end of the business.

And then there's distribution. How will the artist get music into the hands of the fans? Selling CDs out of the trunk of one's car is always an option, although somewhat archaic. Volume becomes problematic, as well. The typical trunk will only house so many CDs between a spare tire and various other paraphernalia. Once again, the Internet comes to the rescue. With relative ease, bands can sell downloadable versions of their music on their website, Facebook, MySpace, Topspin, and so forth. Selling CDs, T-shirts, and other merchandise at live shows and websites is also natural. But more on this later.

Within these pages you won't find much, if anything, about music theory, composition, or becoming a better musician. There are plenty of books and resources available to help you with those points. What you will find is a blueprint for starting your career in music, that is, how to set goals, deal with the business issues, develop a sensible, sound plan for success, and implement action plans.

Also, it should be noted that many of the quotes and references within these pages are related to rock music. It's what I know best, so it's what I write. But the core concepts, tools, and techniques will work for a band or solo artist working in any genre.

So, without further ado, turn the page, and let's get started.

1

Defining and Creating
Success as a Musician

Success is a relative term, and defining it can be somewhat dodgy. For many musicians just starting out, success means becoming the stereotypical rock star, complete with platinum albums, sold-out stadium shows, a mansion on the beach, limos, and party after party. For others, it simply means creating a steady, comfortable living making music. For still others, success means having a day job and playing gigs on the weekends just for fun.

It all comes down to this: Success is how you define it and how you define it for *yourself*. When you allow others to make that decision for you, you can easily set yourself up for a load of pressure and anxiety. Plus, the ironic thing is that even if you attain a level of success, it usually turns out not to be what you thought it would. Then you can find yourself thinking, "I did all that for this? Good grief!"

Success has a lot to do with attitude. Thomas Edison is credited with saying, "I didn't fail 3,000 times. I found 3,000 ways how not to create a light bulb." Whether he actually said it or not (and the numbers vary depending on the version), the point is clear: It's how we approach success and failure that matters. Edison could have thrown in the towel after several attempts, and we'd all still be playing by candlelight.

A close friend of mine played bass with some big names in the early days. It was mostly session work as I recall. Was that success? Perhaps. But today he plays with Christian bands here and there, mostly for fun. When he talks about the session work, his tone is fairly mundane. He gets a bit more excited when he talks about the current band. He also heads up a kid's music ministry at his church. When he talks about that, his eyes sparkle, and you can hear the pride in his voice. To me, that's unmistakable success.

Consider what you are trying to achieve with your music. Give it careful thought. Here are some questions to ponder:

- What does success mean to you? What's your definition of success?
- Picture yourself as successful. What does it look like to you?
- What needs to happen or change for you and your music to become that picture?

No doubt, to some of you this will sound like a silly exercise in futility. Frankly, I've never been big on the whole visualization bit, but what this does is aid in focusing your concept of success. As you go through the questions, you might just find that what you think is important really isn't all that important. As mentioned earlier, our concept of success is usually the result of us buying into society's or some other person's idea of what success should be for us.

Here's a case in point, using myself as the example. By profession, in addition to being a writer, I'm a graphic designer and marketing consultant. When I was young and stupid, I wanted to build a design firm, work on national accounts, travel hither and yon, win awards, make a bunch of money, and do all the stuff usually associated with that life. It was what I learned from others, both personally and through books and articles. That was success to me—at least I thought so. I did all that and found it wasn't all it was cracked up to be in reality. What I thought would be fun and exciting turned into a daily effort to make the overhead, bring in new business, meet impossible deadlines, and perform other anxiety-inducing tasks. For me, it was an abject lesson in "be careful what you wish for, because you just might get it."

The concept of success varies widely among musicians. Emilio Castillo, founder and leader of the highly successful urban soul band Tower of Power, has shared his thoughts about how he defines success: "When people recognize your music by your own personal musical signature. Once you've found your voice, success varies but generally grows exponentially," said Castillo. Lipbone Redding is a New York-based musician with the uncanny ability to use his voice to imitate a trombone. He's also an accomplished soloist, songwriter, guitarist, and entertainer. Redding has noted, "Money is important, but only to the extent that it lets me continue my creative endeavor. Sustainability, as an artist, is a big part of success."

For part-time musician and author/hip-hop historian Sean XLG, success means something perhaps a bit broader. "My goal as a musician is to have the new style of hip-hop music that I created, Adult Contemporary Rap, accepted and embraced by the mainstream world of music. It's an alternative form of rap that primarily appeals to an older, mature audience, whereas the only form of rap currently on the market is youth-oriented. This would be expanding and broadening the genre," said Sean. To some, Sean's definition might sound lofty and unattainable. But without visionaries we'd likely still be living in the Dark Ages, thinking the sun revolved around the Earth. It's the visionaries that allow music to grow, expand, and evolve.

THERE'S NO MAGIC FORMULA

When it comes to success, sorry folks, but there's no magic formula that will make all your hopes and dreams come true. It's going to take a clearly focused plan, sensible, achievable goals, hard work, and a bit of serendipity tossed in for good measure.

The place to start is to do a self-assessment. The typical stumbling block with a self-assessment is being honest. That doesn't mean we set out to blatantly lie to ourselves. Odds are, that annoying little voice in the back of our head will know and call us on the carpet. It simply means that what's in our mind's eye doesn't quite align with reality. In many areas of our life, the way we see and understand things about ourselves isn't the way those traits really are in actuality. It's normal human behavior. We tend to be too close to ourselves to see some things clearly, while others can see these parts of us. So, when doing a self-assessment, it's important to include others. They should be people who know you well and will give an honest opinion. It's been said that a good friend will tell you when you're awesome. A great friend will tell you when you're being an idiot. The hard truth is that it's much better to realize, early on, that you're not cut out to be a professional musician, rather than sink a ton of time, effort, and money into something that will never work out the way you hope.

Here is a set of questions, albeit not exhaustive by any means, to help get you started:

- Do people who know you believe you are well suited to being a professional musician?
- Do you consider yourself a self-starter?
- Do you consider yourself naturally talented?
- Do you have support from family and friends?
- Are you willing to put in the time and effort to continually improve your playing, songwriting, and/or voice?
- Do you have enough confidence in yourself and your abilities to sustain yourself as a professional musician when things get tough?
- Are you prepared, if needed, to lower your standard of living until your musical career is firmly established?
- Do others consider you a team player?
- Do you have the ability to get along with difficult people?
- Are you willing to learn basic business skills?
- Do you manage money well?

Success in the music industry, no matter how you define it, isn't usually an overnight sensation or a get-famous-and-rich-quick thing.

It takes time, effort, work, and a decent dose of patience. You've got to be willing to continually improve your musical abilities, develop your business skills, and hone your showmanship to grow your fan base. Remember, when you're starting out without a manager, an agent, or an A&R person watching your back (and hopefully not putting a knife into it), you're the one who wears all the hats. Be clear and honest with yourself about what you're good at and, perhaps more important, what you stink at doing. You can find people to handle the tasks you don't excel at doing. Sure, it will probably cost you some bucks, but it can be money well spent that significantly helps you project a much more polished, professional image.

SWOT ANALYSIS AND SETTING ATTAINABLE GOALS

Now it's time for a little business lesson. The next step in a self-analysis is conducting a SWOT analysis. That may sound like a big, scary corporate exercise complete with suits and briefcases. Actually, it's nothing more than an honest appraisal of your strengths and weaknesses, along with opportunities that may help you and threats to your success. Typically, strengths and weaknesses are internal (you), while threats and opportunities are external (them).

For example, let's say you are one of those people who are gifted with perfect or relative pitch. If you hear it, you can play it. That's a definite strength. Some say it's a curse, though, because the world is apparently out of tune. On the flip side, maybe you're lousy at improvisation. That could be a weakness, especially if you're into jazz. An opportunity might be bumping into a ridiculously wealthy guy who's into music and looking to invest in a band. If you're a lead guitarist, and guitarists are a dime a dozen in your area . . . and good . . . that would be a threat. You get the idea.

After you've firmly established what success means to you and where your strengths, weaknesses, opportunities, and threats lie, it's time to start putting some goals and objectives together. Goals are broad-based intentions. They make up the big picture. Objectives, on the other hand, are more specific and measurable. The trick with goals is making them attainable. When people make goals that are too lofty, they set themselves up for failure from the beginning, become disappointed, and give up. For example, if you're just starting out, landing a major record deal next month isn't likely to happen. Playing a fund-raiser with a big crowd including some industry movers and shakers just might.

Set goals that will challenge you and then chop them up into smaller, quantifiable objectives that are attainable. Each objective brings you closer to your bigger goals. Working this way will help you stay motivated and focused as you complete each step.

It's also important to remember that goals should not be so firmly set that they trap you in a box. They need to be adaptable and malleable. That was a factor for Brian Doherty, a drummer and music teacher based in New York City. On the topic of goals, he shared the following with me:

> My goals have changed and evolved throughout my career. When I first moved to NYC at the age of 18, my only goal was to get work as a musician. A bit later, my wish was granted, and I got loads of work, most of which were crappy gigs with lousy pay. So much for reaching my goal!
>
> Later, my goals evolved to reflect my wiser, more business-oriented mind-set. They became more about me only taking high-paying work as a drummer and producer. What happened? I stopped getting work altogether. Now, I've refined my goals to [the following]:
>
> 1. Maintain a strong presence in the [music] business for as long as possible.
> 2. Develop and nurture a network from every corner and crevice of the biz.
> 3. Like a slow-burning candle, maintain a steady, even hand in the business as a drummer-for-hire while diversifying my skill set (i.e., teaching, writing, songwriting, producing, and drumming).

4. Create products that generate royalties over [the] long term. Musicians do too much pay-for-play kind of work, while the rest of the business feeds on the financial benefits that musicians provide.

Brian's ability to see the situation for what it was and align his goals with reality was a smart move.

Consider this: Let's say you have a goal to be an in-demand, constantly booked band in your regional area that can command above-average fees for gigs and grow a dedicated fan base of fans who become evangelists for your music. That's a fairly broad and noble goal. It's also a huge chunk to bite off and chew on all at once. Breaking it down into objectives might go something like this:

- Set aside $____ from each performance to be put toward demo production.
- Produce demo, including studio and live recordings, by November 30, 2012.
- Compile a list of booking contacts within the region by April 30, 2012.
- Compile a list of regional media contacts by April 30, 2012.
- Develop press kit by May 15, 2012.
- Have Twitter presence in place and active by June 1, 2012.
- Complete website and Facebook and MySpace pages by July 1, 2012.
- Complete podcast development by July 30, 2012.
- Have street team in place by August 1, 2012.
- Send press kit to booking and media contacts, with demo, by December 15, 2012.
- Follow up, by phone or email, with booking and media contacts by December 21, 2012.

As an independent artist or band seeking to make a career in music, it's critical to remember that this is your job, your livelihood, and a business that will enable you to eat and pay the rent. It's not a hobby. Planning your career is paramount to success.

WHERE DO YOU FIT IN?

The music industry offers a variety of career positions. There are players and performers, arrangers, producers, songwriters, composers, teachers, and more. All are worthy. Each can be extremely rewarding and satisfying. Virtually all of them, however, are highly competitive.

After completing your self-assessment and SWOT analysis, you might find that what you thought you wanted to do isn't the best career path for you. Your skills, talents, and training might be better suited to a different position within the music industry.

CareersInMusic.com is an excellent site to visit for information about the many positions available within the industry. As a matter of fact, the site lists more than 100 roles, complete with descriptions, salary ranges, training and education needed, opportunities for advancement, and more.

The U.S. Bureau of Labor Statistics lists some interesting points about musical careers, several of which will be no surprise. Here are some highlights:[1]

- Part-time schedules—typically at night and on weekends— intermittent unemployment, and rejection when auditioning for work are common; many musicians and singers supplement their income with earnings from other sources.
- Competition for jobs, especially full-time jobs, is keen; talented individuals who can play several instruments and perform a wide range of musical styles should enjoy the best job prospects.
- Full-time musicians with long-term employment contracts, such as those with symphony orchestras or television and film production companies, enjoy steady work and less travel.

- Most instrumental musicians work closely with a variety of other people, including colleagues, agents, employers, sponsors, and audiences.
- Long-term on-the-job training is the most common way people learn to become musicians or singers.
- Formal training may be obtained through private study with an accomplished musician, in a college or university music program, or in a music conservatory. An audition generally is necessary to qualify for university or conservatory study. The National Association of Schools of Music is made up of 615 accredited college-level programs in music. Courses typically include music theory, music interpretation, composition, conducting, and performance (either with a particular instrument or a voice performance). Music directors, composers, conductors, and arrangers need considerable related work experience or advanced training in these subjects.
- Musicians, singers, and related workers held about 240,000 jobs in 2008, of which 186,400 were held by musicians and singers; 53,600 were music directors and composers.
- Around 43 percent worked part-time; 50 percent were self-employed.
- Many found jobs in cities in which entertainment and recording activities are concentrated, such as New York, Los Angeles, Las Vegas, Chicago, and Nashville.
- Of those who earn a wage or salary, 33 percent were employed by religious, grant-making, civic, professional, and similar organizations and 12 percent by performing arts companies, such as professional orchestras, small chamber music groups, opera companies, musical theater companies, and ballet troupes.
- Employment is expected to grow as fast as average.
- Talent alone is no guarantee of success: Many people start out to become musicians or singers but leave the profession because they find the work difficult, the discipline demanding,

STARTING YOUR CAREER AS A MUSICIAN

and the long periods of intermittent unemployment a hardship.

- Median hourly wages of wage-and-salary musicians and singers were $21.24* in May 2008. The middle 50 percent earned between $11.49 and $36.36. The lowest 10 percent earned less than $7.64, and the highest 10 percent earned more than $59.92. Median hourly wages were $23.68 in performing arts companies and $12.50 in religious organizations.
- Median annual wages of salaried music directors and composers were $41,270 in May 2008. The middle 50 percent earned between $26,480 and $63,200. The lowest 10 percent earned less than $16,750, and the highest 10 percent earned more than $107,280.
- It is rare for musicians and singers to have guaranteed employment that exceeds 3 to 6 months.
- Because they may not work steadily for one employer, some performers cannot qualify for unemployment compensation and few have typical benefits such as sick leave or paid vacations.

Does that sound somewhat bleak and meant to scare the heck out of you? Absolutely! But it's far better to know what you're getting yourself into at the beginning, rather than find yourself playing for tips in a park or on the sidewalk to make ends meet.

THE ELUSIVE TRAIT CALLED "DRIVE"

The *Oxford American Dictionary* carries several definitions of the word *drive*. As a verb, it's defined as "to propel or carry by force along a specified direction," or as "to work to an excessive extent." As a noun, *drive* is defined as "the determination and ambition of a person to achieve something." If we put those together, we come up with a

---

* All dollar amounts mentioned in the book refer to the U.S. dollar (USD).

definition something along the lines of "the ambition of person to achieve something (a musical career, in this case), propelled and carried by sheer force of will and hard work." That can be whittled down to a simpler concept: If you truly believe in yourself, in your talent and value as a musician, never take no for an answer. In the words of Jon Bon Jovi, "Success is falling nine times and getting up ten."[2]

Being successful requires drive and also a very targeted focus on what you're trying to accomplish. When you lose focus and lose sight of your goal, you lose. Period. If you find you'd rather do battle with the PlayStation than practice and rehearse, it might be time to think of a different career path.

Lots of people in all sorts of professions know what they need to do to be successful, yet they don't do it for a variety of reasons. It might seem too tough. It could be fear. They simply might be too lazy. They may think they don't have the resources, and rather than find alternate ways to find those resources, they just give up.

To sum up, you might be the most talented player around, but without the drive and ambition to back it up, unfortunately, it means little.

DEFINING YOUR MUSIC

In business, there's a thing called an elevator pitch. It's a short blurb you say when somebody asks you what you do. Typically, people respond with their job title: "I'm an accountant," "I'm a photographer," "I play in a band." The problem with these responses is that they're not engaging, or, worse, they're utterly boring. They do nothing to open a dialogue with the other person.

The trick is to think of words and phrases that truly describe your music, particularly if you play originals. These descriptions should be brief but capture the attention of the other person—something along the lines of (and this is a stretch), "Our music is like the intersection where Metallica meets Jewel." The other person should come away thinking, "Wow! I need to hear that." Of course, this is much easier said than done.

The words you use to describe your music need to be tightly honed and so appealing as to encourage people to do something—buy/download a tune or a ticket, tell a friend, and so forth. Don't leave this to chance. If you're in a band, talk to your mates. Agree on what to say and be consistent. Painful? Sure. Sometimes it can be a challenge to agree on things. But it is nonetheless necessary. This will become a core element of your brand, which will be discussed more in chapter 3.

The ability to accurately describe your music will go miles toward positioning your act. Positioning is one of those terms used by the suits in marketing. It simply means where your brand—your band or act—fits in the minds of the fans, media, and other influencers. People like to pigeonhole all sorts of things. Let them. It makes it easier for them to think about various bands and put them in a nice, tidy box. There will be plenty of opportunity to spread your musical wings after you've established yourself.

Eclectic musician Frank Zappa was known for creating music that was often difficult, if not impossible, to categorize. For the majority of his fans, he was known as a rocker who wrote some pretty avant-garde stuff that was unique. That was his commercial positioning. Yet few likely knew that Zappa was also a classical composer, particularly later in life. The point is that your positioning isn't necessarily the only type of music you perform or write—but it is what you promote.

During the British Invasion of the early 1960s, The Beatles were positioned as the nice boys from Liverpool. Sure, they had long hair and sang, "Yeah, yeah, yeah." But, they were still the nice young chaps you wouldn't really mind your daughter dating. The Rolling Stones, on the other hand, were the bad boys of rock and roll. They were more than a wee bit on the scary and dangerous side. The positioning fit both bands and worked well.

THE IMPORTANCE OF DEVELOPING A PLAN

I've mentioned planning a lot so far. But what should your plan include, and how do you put it together? A fair question. A plan is, by definition, a detailed proposal for doing or achieving something. It's like a road map you use to guide your direction and decisions, while providing a measuring stick for your success or missteps.

Developing a clear, well-thought-out, and sensible plan can, almost automatically, put you ahead of the pack. That's because the pack didn't take the time and effort to draft one. They simply let their musical career happen to them, rather than taking control of their destiny. Sure, they have hopes, dreams, and hazy ideas, but they have nothing in writing that will hold them accountable and responsible for realizing those high-minded hopes.

It's important to remember that a plan isn't meant to stifle your creativity or be a spontaneity crusher. It's not selling out or boxing you into a concrete container. A good plan is flexible and should be malleable, based on current circumstances, while still guiding you where you want to go. While music is art, professionally, it's also a business, and your career should be treated as such.

By now, perhaps you have some goals and objectives. You may have defined your musical niche and your fans. That's a place to start. A band that sounds like Metalocalypse's Dethklok is going to have a reasonably different plan from somebody who sounds like Woody Guthrie. There may be some common points, but the specifics will, and should, vary in order to successfully reach and impact their audience of fans, influencers, booking agents, and such.

Developing your plan will be addressed in detail in chapter 3. But, for now, here are some of the components of a typical plan:

- Executive summary: This is an overview of the entire plan. Think of it as the highlights and major points.
- Goals: As mentioned, define what you are trying accomplish and why.
- Define the band identity: What is your band or individual act all about? Who and what are you in the minds of your audience? Or, what are you trying to be? This should also include your desired positioning in your public's eyes.

- Marketing and promotion overview: How are you going to get the word out and get your music on the audience's radar screens? What tools and resources will be needed to accomplish that effort?

- Audience/fan profile: Who are they, and what's important to them? The more you can learn about your fans, the better. Don't try to be all things to all people. When folks do, they often end up becoming nothing to everybody because there's no differentiation. It all begins to sound the same, and there's no compelling reason for the audience to listen to you over all the other bands.

- Competition: Learn all you can about those other guys and gals who are breathing down your neck, vying for the same gig. What are their strengths and weaknesses? What are their marketing efforts like? This should include a review of their music, of course, but also their Internet presence, merchandise, posters, live shows, and so forth. The more you can find out, the better.

- Revenue sources: Savvy musicians leverage their assets to maximize revenue and profit. Sound capitalistic? It is. But being a starving artist, for the most part, stinks. You might not get rich and famous, but making a comfortable living while doing what you love sure beats living in a cardboard box along some forgotten alley. Some revenue sources include original music, live shows, digital downloads, merchandise such as T-shirts, and CDs. There are also potential opportunities for licensing and selling your tunes to various commercial applications, or for writing and playing music for games, theater, broadcast, and so on.

- Action/promotion plans: These are your objectives. It's where you detail how you're going to reach your goals. Your action plans might address these points:
  - Print, including flyers, posters, business cards, and so forth.

□ The Internet, including your band's website, blog, and social media

□ Public relations and networking

□ Developing a press kit

□ Live show development: What will you do on stage that is unique, has impact, engages the audience, and is memorable? Also consider whether you'll need props and special equipment. This section can also cover your strategy for playing benefits to gain recognition and similar venues.

• Merchandise: Merchandise is stuff you sell at shows and can give away as a promotional tool. The typical stuff includes CDs, T-shirts, and posters. But why not get imaginative and stretch yourself a bit? How about a USB drive with your band's logo and a few tunes on it? Key chain bottle openers can be a hit as can beer koozies. Nobody likes a warm beer at a show. These are also called premium items, and most are dirt-cheap to buy but can be sold at a nice profit.

• Budget: This is exactly what it sounds like. How much money is it going to cost you to jump-start and continue your marketing and promotional efforts? You don't need all the money at once. A percentage of show fees and other revenue sources can be put aside to fund your efforts over time.

Beyond this, it's important to plan how you're going to deal with money. How will you get paid, and what does that money go toward? The band members need to be paid. There might also be others, such as a manager, agent, PR person, and so on, who want their slice of the pie. Plus, there's equipment to buy or rent, maintain, and repair beyond the dollars earmarked for marketing and promotion. As you become more successful, you can count on more outstretched hands wanting their share.

• Marketing calendar: When you complete your plan, or at least have a solid draft, it's a good idea to create a marketing calendar to help keep you on track. You'll know what needs to be done and by when and how much money needs to be put aside to make it all happen. Google Calendars is a handy tool for this. It's free and, because it's Internet-based, it can easily be shared among the band members and other key people. You can find it at www.google.com/calendar.

2

Your Musical Education

It should come as no surprise that a musical education starts early for most. For some, it's a labor. For others, it's instinctive and intuitive. In my case, it was a labor and one that I utterly abhorred. I started playing piano when I was roughly seven or eight years old. Fortunately, over time, I've managed to successfully block much of the trauma from my memory.

Like most kids around my age at the time, I wanted to learn Beatles tunes. I wanted to don a mop-top wig while singing, "Yeah, yeah, yeah." My teachers, however, wanted me to learn classical compositions, assorted theory, scales, and chord progressions. I had one teacher who would smack my hands when I screwed up. I had another who believed bribery was an acceptable teaching method.

Although her name escapes me, she was a little old lady who, once each week, would show up at our front door loaded to the hilt with thermal picnic bags. Inside was a confectionary feast that would make Willy Wonka proud. When I successfully plunked out a tune, I received some candy as a reward. I think she may have been in league with my dentist.

This went on for several years. Apparently, I was supposed to be attaining culture, refinement, and an appreciation of the arts. What I actually received was a headache, in three-quarter time, for one hour each and every misery-ridden day between lessons and practice. But at least the candy lady didn't smash my fingers.

My son, on the other hand, is one of those instinctive players. If he hears it, he can play it. And he can play it on pretty much whatever instrument happens to be close by. His gift, it would seem, did not emerge from my part of the gene pool.

My son began his musical education in the fifth grade, playing trumpet. We were fortunate to live in a school district that valued music and the arts, along with sports. He learned to read music, studied theory, honed his ear, and mastered the practical bits about making a pleasant sound come out of that horn. In a short time, he became first chair for trumpet in his school orchestra.

When he was thirteen, I started to teach him to play guitar. It was the usual fare—basic chords, twelve-bar blues, and such. Within three months, he was tapping, playing sweep arpeggios, and moving up and down the fretboard with amazing speed and accuracy.

How did he do it? Practice . . . and YouTube. He would practice for roughly four hours each day. He'd pour over YouTube videos to learn a particular technique. The point here is that this stuff doesn't just happen, in most cases. It takes dedication, time, and a willingness to screw up, learn from your mistakes, and start again.

Guitarist Florian Opahle started her musical education very early on. It's paid off. She began working with Jethro Tull front man Ian Anderson in his solo band and orchestral projects.

I started with musical pre-education at the age of four. . . . At the age of five I picked up the guitar and had lessons in classical guitar until the age of twenty. Also, when I was twelve, I started taking electric guitar lessons. At the age of eighteen, I began the first recording and live sessions for various artists in different studios here in Germany.

While on the road with a female singer called "Masha," we had the great chance to open up a tour for Jethro Tull as a support act. That is how I met Ian Anderson. He then later offered me [the chance] to play guitar in the Ian Anderson plays the Orchestral Jethro Tull Tour. A dream came true!

Opahle, Anderson, and company toured Europe and the United States with a full orchestra, the Neue Philharmonie Frankfurt, conducted by John O'Hara; the show has been captured as a DVD release.

FORMAL TRAINING OR THE SEAT OF YOUR PANTS METHOD?

When it comes to learning music, there are plenty of methods. Being self-taught is the method many start with. That's how I started with guitar. I bought my first guitar without having a clue how to play a note, let alone an entire chord. I bought a few guitar magazines and some sheet music and tried to make sense out of it. My piano background helped a bit. At least I had some sort of a reference point to begin with.

I'd listen to records and try my best to pick out the songs. Frankly, I wasn't very good at it. But I had a secret weapon. My best friend, who, like my son, can play anything, was just a phone call away. Actually, I think he was at my house more than his own, so that was pretty handy. All I needed to do was ask, "Hey, how does that tune go?" He'd guide me through. It's similar for many musicians. They have friends, band mates, or others who will take pity on their poor, clueless souls and teach them this song and that.

Learning from other musicians is a typical path and, arguably, the path taken by most professionals. As mentioned, there might be some background from classes at school, but learning various techniques, songs, arrangements, and so forth is how many musicians hone their skills.

Defining the terms *self-taught* and *formal education* can be a bit nebulous. *Self-taught* is usually defined as just that—picking up an instrument and figuring out how to make music with it. That's often backed up with the input of other musicians, friends, and such.

These days, musicians have the benefit of learning tunes, techniques, and more via YouTube videos. Many well-known artists freely share their tools of the trade to help out others. Plus, because it's Internet-based, this type of learning can be done on your own schedule, whether it be your desktop, laptop, tablet, or other device.

But what if you can't find another musician or teacher? That was the problem for Natalia Paruz, also known as "The Saw Lady." Playing the saw is pretty unusual, and finding instruction can be more than a challenge.

Originally trained as a professional dancer, Natalia was a trainee with New York's noted Martha Graham Contemporary Dance Company. All that changed in an instant. When asked about her path into the music industry and education, she shared,

> One day, on my way back from Lincoln Center, I was hit by a taxi cab. That put an end to my dance career. To cheer me up, my parents took me on a trip to Europe, and in a show for tourists I saw a guy playing a musical saw. That was the first time since the accident that I felt excited about something other than dance, and it started my musical career. I was attracted not only to the mesmerizing sound but also to the visual—it is one of the only instruments where the entire instrument moves when one plays it, so it's like a dance! . . .
>
> When I was in elementary school, I learned to play recorder, piano, and guitar. I sang in a choir, and I learned music theory. But I wasn't serious about it. When I wanted to learn to play the saw, I discovered that there were no teachers to be found, so I was forced to be self-taught. As a result, I developed my own technique, which enabled me to play louder, faster, and more accurately than other saw players.

Natalia's dedication to learn her newfound instrument has opened the door for several other opportunities and activities. She notes, "I founded a festival, the NYC Musical Saw Festival, now in its tenth year (www.MusicalSawFestival.org). The festival promotes the musical instrument I play. Instead of being in competition with other people who play the same instrument I do, I bring them together. There is more power in joined forces.

"Also, I organized a Guinness World Record for the Largest Musical Saw Ensemble. We broke the previous record of twenty-eight musical saw players that was made in Poland with fifty-five musical saw players in NYC. This got us world[wide] acclaim and recognition." I don't know about you, but my hat is off to Ms. Paruz. She's quite a remarkable woman and musician.

Private instruction is another typical method. The trick is finding a teacher who knows his or her stuff and is someone you can get along with and respect. After I bought that first guitar, I signed up for lessons at the music store where I purchased it. It seemed a logical thing to do. As for my teacher, in retrospect, I'm sure he was a nice enough guy, but as a kid I couldn't relate to him at all. He seemed to me, at the time, to have one foot in the grave and the other on a banana peel. By the third lesson he uttered that fateful word: "recital." That was it. I was done and out of there.

Nonetheless, private music instruction brings with it many benefits. You choose the teacher. In many cases, lessons are held in your home. Probably the biggest benefit, though, is the ability to learn at your own pace. Who knows—you might even get lucky and score some candy like I did.

For many professional musicians, the start of their education was elementary or secondary music classes, band, or orchestra. Teachers are something of the luck of the draw and dependent on the wisdom of the school administration. As mentioned, my son was fortunate not only to attend a school system that values the arts but also to have an extraordinary music teacher and music program director. Many these days are not so fortunate. Music and the arts, despite their proven benefits, are often the first things cut from the budget when money gets tight.

Here comes the obligatory anecdote. I took music theory in high school. I figured it would be a breeze. Boy, was I wrong. It made calculus look like a walk in the park. It was, without a doubt, the single most difficult class I took that year, or any year during my high school career, for that matter. Transposition from piano to a B–flat clarinet? Consonance and dissonance? Serial composition and set theory? Huh? I was utterly lost.

But there was a bright side. Our teacher took us into Manhattan, back in the early 1970s, for a field trip. You know . . . when New York was New York . . . gritty and dangerous. Here was this delightful young blonde music theorist towing, en masse, a group of adolescent pseudo-hippies through the streets of Manhattan, in the dark of night, to listen to Michael Tilson Thomas perform John Cage.

For the unenlightened, Michael Tilson Thomas is an American conductor, pianist, and composer. He is currently music director of the San Francisco Symphony, and artistic director of the New World Symphony Orchestra. John Gage was an American composer and a pioneer of indeterminacy in music, electroacoustic music, and nonstandard use of musical instruments. Cage was one of the leading figures of the postwar avant-garde. Critics have lauded him as one of the most influential American composers of the 20th century.

Our group of about twenty-five or so was joined by another twenty-five or thirty folks as the performance began. All of us were seated on the floor of a second-floor room in an old building. It was a small venue, and the orchestra, rather more of an ensemble, consisted of maybe five or six players. I had no idea where I was or what to expect.

What I heard that evening was like nothing I'd ever heard before. Absolutely nothing. The piano was retro-fitted with cans, wood blocks, and other assorted noise-making items for the hammers to hit. I'm not even sure what they did with the percussion instruments.

At one point, the music stopped, and Tilson Thomas went over and opened a window. The sounds of New York City rushed in. It was part of the composition. The whole experience was weird in a strange, yet exhilarating, way.

There was a gentleman seated cross-legged in the row in front of me. He was in his late sixties, I'd say. He had long white hair and a rather bushy white beard. He looked something like Santa Claus in denim. Tilson Thomas introduced him as the composer. I was stunned. Apparently, so was Cage, because he appeared rather . . . er . . . "happy," in a glazed kind of way.

The point of this little anecdote is to keep your eyes open and your ears open even more. There are things around us that will enhance our musical education and provide inspiration. It might be a sound, a piece of art or architecture, or a conversation. Not all music is about the topics usually found in the Top 40. Music is about enjoying melodies but also about making us think.

Chicago–based singer and songwriter Anna Fermin took a bit of a hybrid approach to learning music. "I took formal piano and violin lessons throughout grade school and junior high and sung in the concert and show choirs in high school," said Fermin. She added, "When I started writing my own music, after college, I taught myself how to play acoustic guitar, which is what I've used to write my songs until the last couple [of] years. Now I mostly write on the piano."

For those seeking a musical career, a college or university-level education might be in order. This is especially important—actually mandatory—for classical musicians and music teachers, as well as other positions in the field. While many universities and colleges offer music majors and advanced musical degrees, the schools that often come to mind are Juilliard, the Manhattan School of Music, and Berklee. These schools offer a broad array of curriculum in addition to instrument studies. For example, Juilliard offers Ear Training and Principles of Harmony, along with a variety of Liberal Arts courses.

Wendy Hayes is a jazz vocalist based in Asheville, North Carolina, whose path took her through higher education. Wendy noted, "I have a Bachelor's and Master's in Vocal Performance from Appalachian State University. I studied opera and only recently discovered a passion for singing jazz. I have been attending jazz workshops, working on my own, and conferring with other jazz musicians. Jazz is largely an aural tradition, so that goes a long way in being authentic. Of course, book knowledge never hurt anyone either, and I do love to study."

Drummer Brian Doherty works as both a professional musician and a music teacher. He said, "I'm formally educated in music and education. I have a Master's and Bachelor's of Music from the Manhattan School of Music. I also have a Master's of Education from the City College of New York. However, I am completely self-taught in the area of business."

As mentioned, many musical positions require a formal college or university-level education. But I find it interesting that in his study, *Formal and Informal Music Learning: Attitudes and Perspectives of Secondary School Non-Music Teachers,* Dr. John L. Vitale found that the forty-one participants, all non-music teachers from a suburban Toronto, Canada, area high school, placed a high value on informally trained musicians. From the study's abstract:

> Data collection includes a questionnaire based on a semantic dif-
> ferential scale, as well as a randomly selected focus group. Hence,
> this is a mixed method study integrating both quantitative and
> qualitative data. Results indicate that the attitudes and perspec-
> tives of the participants were very positive towards informally
> trained musicians. Specifically, participants generated three prin-
> cipal themes. The first theme of value indicates that informally
> trained musicians are very esteemed members of society. The
> second theme of creativity identifies how informally trained
> musicians are great composers. Lastly, the theme of non-confor-
> mity focuses on the steadfast desire of informally trained musi-
> cians to achieve musical competency without formal instruc-
> tion. From an education perspective, conclusions demonstrate
> that formal music educators should consider the inherent advan-
> tages of informal music learning.[3]

This begs the question: Is the investment of both time and money worth it for the aspiring professional musician? Once again, it depends on a musician's career goals. For someone seeking a position with a professional orchestra, the answer is a resounding "yes." But for people who are seeking to play clubs or write, perform, and record pop or rock music, they'll probably be better off saving their money by going the informal route.

As a matter of fact, nearly all the professional musicians I spoke with while doing the research for this book were informally trained, and none of them felt it hurt their career. Many actually felt it enhanced their career. They didn't feel tied to various rules, so they had a wider range of creative expression to pull from. Their classically or formally trained counterparts often didn't have that same sense of creative expression playing someone else's compositions.

That's not to say formal training stifles creativity. The formally trained musician has the opportunity to interpret a composition. Consider artists such as cellist Yo Yo Ma, who received his formal musical education at such notable schools as Harvard University, Juilliard, and Columbia University. He's won several Grammy Awards and received other honors, including the Presidential Medal of Freedom and the National Medal of Arts. One doesn't achieve this type of notoriety simply by playing note for note. Yo Yo Ma brings elegance and grace to his musical interpretations. Preeminent violinist Itzhak Perlman is similar in this regard, as is pianist, conductor, and composer André Previn.

Conversely, Black Sabbath front man Ozzy Osbourne said in an interview that he had no idea what key he sang in and couldn't tell one end of a sheet of music from the other. In a 1980 *Playboy Magazine* interview, John Lennon is credited with saying, "None of us could read music. None of us can write it." Yet Lennon and Paul McCartney went on to write some of the most memorable songs of the 20th century.

So, it all comes down to those goals. What are you trying to accomplish with your music? To reach your career goals, does it make sense to invest in a formal education, or like Lennon and McCartney, does your music emanate from your heart and soul, even though you may not know the difference between a whole note and a quarter note? The only one who can answer those questions is you. Take the time needed to develop crystal-clear goals, and the rest will fall into place.

Beyond studies, the college and university environment is conducive to music, bands, and performance. Many well-known groups got their start on a campus. R.E.M., Radiohead, Pink Floyd, and Coldplay all trace their roots to a college, as do the Talking Heads at the Rhode Island School of Design, Public Enemy at Adelphi University, and Devo at Kent State University. Tapping into the college music market, both for performances and radio, will be addressed later in this book.

3

Your Band's Brand and Marketing

At some point, if you're serious, the time will come when you're ready to move your band out of the garage and get on stage, into the recording studio, and into the public eye. You've practiced. You've rehearsed your stage performance. You've worked hard to hone your act and define your sound. One thing you probably haven't done is given some serious thought to branding and marketing.

Don't sweat it. It's not that unusual. Your focus has been on the music, improving your playing, and getting all the band's members to play nice together (I'm not talking about the music bits). That's the way it should be. Before you can even think about branding and marketing, you've got to have something to brand and market—something viable. That might sound like an obvious statement, but all too often small businesses try to brand something that's not quite there yet. Their branding, if it's even addressed, is all over the place and utterly inconsistent. Then their efforts fail, and they think branding doesn't work or isn't needed. As I've mentioned, your band is a small business. Sure, music might be your product, but the general business concepts are the same. As a business, you've got a brand.

WHAT IS BRANDING?

Branding is another one of those nebulous marketing terms; you've probably heard about it, but aren't too clear on what it means. Take solace in the fact that you're hardly alone. You might think that a brand relates to things such as chain restaurants, detergent, or any number of consumer products and services. While that's true, it also relates to your band. Like it or not, and whether or not you choose to develop it, you have a brand. How well it's defined in the minds of your fans and other audiences is up to you.

The big question is, "What the heck is this branding stuff?" Ask ten people and, chances are, you'll get ten different answers. The American Marketing Association, via Wikipedia (en.wikipedia.org/wiki/Brand), offers us this explanation: "The American Marketing Association defines a *brand* as a 'name, term, design, symbol, or any other feature that identifies one seller's goods or services as distinct from those of other sellers.' A brand's assets can take many forms, including a name, sign, symbol, color combination, or slogan. For example, Coca Cola is the name of a brand made by a particular company."

The concept of branding began during the old Norse period, by means of a red-hot iron stamp, as a way to tell one person's cattle from another's. The word *brand* has continued to evolve to encompass identity—it affects the personality of a product, company, or service. It is defined by a perception, good or bad, that your customers or prospects have about you.

That last line is important. Being "defined by a perception" means that even though it's your act or band and you own the brand assets such as your logo, you don't really own your brand. It's really owned by your audience, and it lives in their minds. It's their perception of your band or solo act.

Your brand is significantly more than your logo. It's the audience's expectation of your music, sound, stage presence, and more. In fact, your brand encompasses every touch point, meaning wherever you interact with your fans, broader audience, and key influencers such as the media, recording industry personnel, and others. That's certainly not something to be left to chance. It requires careful thought, asking tough questions, planning, and consistent implementation.

Let's look at some of those tough questions. These are just a starting point for you:

- What is your music all about? What are you trying to say and accomplish with it?
- Who is your audience? How are they defined?
- What is your audience's attitude? What are they looking for in music?
- What does your band do differently than all the others?
- What bands or acts do you directly compete with in your musical arena? What are they all about in terms of strengths and weaknesses?
- What major problem does your music and act solve for the audience and fans?

    This might sound like a weird question, but music does solve various problems for people. It might be that your songs speak to the hearts and emotions of your audience and reflect their feelings. In effect, your tunes give them an outlet and sense of association or belonging. It may be that your act helps them vent some rage or simply escape for awhile. Conversely, it may help them relax. Maybe you're a cover band that plays oldies. In that case, perhaps your music brings back fond memories for your fans.

- What have your fans gained that they didn't have before listening to you?

    This is the "What's in it for me?" factor and closely related to the previous bullet point. Everybody wants to know what's in it for them. Maybe it's just that, as a species, we're selfish. Each time a fan or other person listens to your songs, leaves a show, buys a T-shirt, and so on, they come away with something more. What is it? Finding the answer goes a long way toward gaining a clear understanding of your fans and audience-at-large.

- What do your fans always expect from you?

It might be a certain sound or type of music. Maybe it's the type of lyrics. It could also be a killer stage show. For example, I can't think of a single Iron Maiden fan who wouldn't be severely disappointed if Eddy didn't show up in some way, shape, or form.

The point is that your audience is expecting something when they listen to you or see your live performance. This is a good question to ask your fans directly. Why guess when you can simply ask?

- What is it that you always do and want to be known for, both musically and with your stage presence?

   This might also cross over into other areas such as political viewpoints or various social commentaries and causes. It can also be a stage experience that's tightly tied to the music. Bob Dylan was known for social and political commentary. So are many other acts. David Bowie was known for creating characters such as Ziggy Stardust, Major Tom, and the Thin, White Duke. KISS, well, that kind of goes without saying: rock and roll, makeup, spewing fake blood, fire here and there, and costuming that was just a bit over the top.

- What is one thing that your band and music stand for?

   If a fan comes away with one thought after hearing you, what would you like it to be? That can be a tough question. For me, the thought that comes to mind about Billy Joel is "brilliantly entertaining songwriter and performer." For Ozzy, it's "Whoa! What fun! That guy's crazy (and appears to be on a train)." For Meatloaf it's "This is theater, this is spectacle, and it's great!"

PUTTING BRANDING INTO ACTION

Developing a name and logo for your band is the first step in your branding efforts. Coming up with a catchy, memorable name that truly reflects what your band and music is about is no small task. As a matter of fact, it can be gut-wrenching. Finding a name—the right name—can also bring with it several other not-so-happy experiences, including fear of choosing the wrong name, apprehension, worry, foreboding, and the ever-popular trepidation. Sounds delightful, doesn't it? It comes with the territory and, hopefully, it will be a one-time exercise, but it's often not.

If you're a solo performer, it's pretty straightforward. It's usually your name or a stage name. For example, Davie Bowie is actually David Robert Jones. He chose the name Bowie based on the American knife and, as he's noted as saying, "a medium for a conglomerate statements and illusions." But the main reason was the fact that a young and upcoming actor, Davy Jones, was already using the same name; he would go on to become famous as the lead singer of the Monkees. Elton John's real name is Reginald Kenneth Dwight. While that's a fine British name, it's not very memorable or catchy. Madonna's full name is Madonna Louise Ciccone. She simply chose to drop the middle name and surname on her way to becoming a music icon.

When it comes to a name for a band, things can get a bit trickier. Band members all have opinions, ideas, and egos. Plus, there's the matter of finding the right moniker or combination of words that will announce what the band is about, can be trademarked and, hopefully, will work with a top-level domain name for a website. To help spur your naming efforts, here's a brief list of band names, along with how they were developed, courtesy of our friends at Wikipedia. (For more, visit en.wikipedia.org/wiki/List_of_band_name_etymologies.)

- AC/DC: Malcolm and Angus Young developed the idea for the band's name after seeing "AC/DC" on an electric sewing machine.
- Alice Cooper: Alice Cooper was a band before one of its members started a solo career under the same name. Allegedly, Alice Cooper was the name of a spirit with whom members of the band came in contact through a Ouija board.
- The Doors: The band took its name from Aldous Huxley's book *The Doors of Perception*, the title of which was a reference to a

William Blake quotation: "When the doors of perception are cleansed, things will appear to man as they truly are . . . infinite."
- Grateful Dead: The name Grateful Dead was chosen from a dictionary. According to Phil Lesh, in his biography, "Jerry Garcia picked up an old Britannica World Language Dictionary . . . [and] in that silvery elf-voice he said to me, 'Hey, man, how about the Grateful Dead?'" The definition there was "the soul of a dead person, or his angel, showing gratitude to someone who, as an act of charity, arranged their burial."
- Queen: They were originally called Smile. Singer Freddie Mercury came up with the new name for the band, later saying, "Years ago I thought up the name 'Queen.' . . . It's just a name, but it's very regal, obviously, and it sounds splendid. . . . It's a strong name, very universal and immediate. It had a lot of visual potential and was open to all sorts of interpretations. I was certainly aware of gay connotations, but that was just one face of it."
- The Rolling Stones: Their name was taken from the Muddy Waters song "Mannish Boy."[4]

DEVELOPING A LOGO FOR YOUR BAND OR SOLO ACT

Once you've settled on a name, designing the band's logo, also called a mark, is the next logical step. In many ways, a logo is the band's face before the public. As such, there are some considerations to keep in mind. A logo should be unique, immediately recognizable, easily read, and reflective of the band's brand image.

Plus, a logo must be scalable, meaning it can be reduced or enlarged without a loss in quality. The best way to achieve this is by creating the logo as a vector graphic. Vector graphics are rendered from a mathematical formula that defines the logo. Vector graphics, in most cases, are created as Adobe Illustrator, .eps, or FreeHand files. The free, open-source application Inkscape will also create vectors. Photoshop, on the other hand, creates bitmapped or raster images that are based on pixels per inch or other units of measurement. They cannot be scaled without a loss in quality, especially when scaled up. In other words, if you have your act's logo created in Photoshop and try to make it larger than the original size, it will look like garbage.

Another consideration is giving thought to how the mark will be reproduced. A good logo is as effective in black and white as it is in color. Many logo designers will work up the designs in black and white first. The idea is that if a mark doesn't work well in black and white, color won't help it. Also, there will be many instances where a one-color or black-and-white version is required. These include silk screening on T-shirts or novelty items, newspaper ads, one-color posters, and so on.

Start by getting some inspiration from the logos of well-known bands and solo performers. A web search for "band logos" will yield some starting points. Of course, you'll also want to review your competition's logos. How do various logos reflect a band's branding? How do the letterforms, symbols, colors, and other elements work together? Do they provide a clue about a band's music and attitude?

The next big question is whether to design your logo yourself or hire a professional designer. Perhaps you have a friend, fan, or other acquaintance who can create a professional-level design. You might luck out and have a band member who's adept at graphics. Such was the case with the iconic KISS logo, which was designed by guitarist Ace Frehley.

A professional logo designer can be expensive, but using one can be money well spent. A good designer will ensure that the selected design is an authentic reflection of the band's identity and branding. Usually the designer will also provide you with a range of file formats, in both black and white and color, that will reproduce well in a variety of instances. Many designers will also include a style guide for the logo that shows how it's built, colors, fonts, and other technical details.

YOUR BRAND IS MORE THAN JUST A LOGO

But your brand is more than a name and a logo. Your band needs to become the entire "package" and work to fulfill fan expectations.

Those expectations encompass the band's sound, music and lyrics, stage presence, and appearance or "look," along with its overall attitude. This "package" is expressed in more obvious things such as printed material, including business cards, posters, and other marketing materials.

Defining your band's sound is another one of those gut-wrenching exercises that are central to branding. What the heck is a "sound," anyway? A fair question that's dodgy, at best, to define. Let's define it as the elusive element that separates your music from everybody else. It's a somewhat abstract quality of music yet is often readily identifiable with a certain band or solo artist.

For example, Queen played an eclectic mix of music, from the iconic "Bohemian Rhapsody" to "Love of My Life" to "I'm in Love with My Car." Although these songs are very different, when you hear them, you immediately think, "Queen." That's because they all carry the signature Queen sound. I once saw an interview with Brian May in which he described the band's sound as "big." It's something they pulled off seamlessly with dynamic harmonies, layer on layer of tracks, Mercury's unique voice, and May's distinctive guitar style. It's thick, meaty, and unmistakably Queen.

Consider guitarists such as Eric Clapton, Carlos Santana, Jeff Beck, B.B. King, and a myriad of others. Their playing style is readily identifiable. How they developed that sound is another complex story.

If your focus is being a wedding band or doing covers, note for note, a unique sound isn't necessary. It can actually be a deterrent. The audience is expecting some decent dance music or a song that sounds exactly like one of their favorite groups. This is where we go back to revisit your goals and what you and your band are trying to accomplish.

When working out your sound, there are a few approaches. One approach is to take the time to become an educated, accomplished player. Obviously, this is a goal every musician should strive to reach. A person might be formally educated, self-taught, or a combination of the two. Someone can play all kinds of music and imitate almost any well-known musician but actively choose not to do so. This type of artist arranges songs, solos, leads, and riffs to express a personal musical point of view. The musician adds bits of this and that, until it feels right. It's a "know-it-in-your-gut" kind of thing. The point is that this person has the musical background and experience to take this approach and do it right so that the music becomes something the artist owns. A cover song isn't necessarily played note for note. It becomes the artist's interpretation of that particular tune.

Another approach is to not listen to anything else but one's own music. The idea is to avoid influences and not become tainted. It's difficult, at best, to pull this off. Isolation usually isn't the best option for a musical career.

At times, achieving a sound simply happens by accident, but it can also be designed, worked on, and refined through a conscious effort. Whether you choose to proactively develop a sound or let it evolve on its own, the idea is to have something unique when all is said and done—something that you own, can be identified with you, and will resonate with your fans. Again, it's often that in-your-gut thing that feels and sounds right with the performer. Then, those musical accents are repeated in other tunes, ultimately becoming a "style," or sound. It's not so much musical, as in repeating riffs, as it is a stylistic way of playing. When it happens and is done well, it becomes something of a musical trademark.

Another important element of your musical brand is your stage presence. Fans expect to see a show when they shell out some money for a ticket. Otherwise, they'd just listen to your tunes in the comfort of their home or car.

What you do on stage and how you do it should be memorable. You want the audience to leave wanting more and thinking, "Whoa! That was amazing!" That's going to require thought, planning, and maybe tapping into some resources for props, special equipment, and so on. Your stage presence and show don't need to rival a major Alice Cooper theatrical production, but your show should be more than you just standing there crooning out some lyrics about love gone wrong or what's wrong with society.

YouTube is handy to generate performance ideas without breaking the bank buying concert tickets. Nonetheless, seeing various artists' live shows is also important. What do these acts do on stage? How do they interact with and engage the audience?

Lighting equipment can get expensive pretty quickly, but it can also give your show an inviting and exciting edge. Fog machines and similar equipment can lend some atmosphere to a show and enhance the lighting. But, even with the most state-of-the-art equipment, if there's no personality on stage, the show will be weak.

While on stage performing, you and the band members have a completely different perspective than the audience, even, and maybe especially, if you're standing next to the other performers. You need to see what your show looks like and hear what it sounds like from the audience's point of view. Consider videotaping your performances. You might start out with rehearsals and then tape live performances. It's tough to develop a good show when you can't see what the audience sees. You might think the singer is looking like a million bucks from the back, but the audience might think he or she is looking somewhat lame.

Without some solid way to gauge what you, your band members, and front person or singer do on stage, all you can do is guess. "Gee, that kick looked cool." Does it really? Without a video or trusted person to tell you how you come off while performing, you're pretty much clueless.

Beyond the stage show is the band's overall "look" and attitude. Are you going for edgy and dark? Innocent and pure? Sexy and sultry? Something in between? What you wear, your hair style, and all the other parts of your public persona should be reviewed to ensure consistency with your band's brand. The members of KISS were masters at this. Up until 1983, they *never* made an official public appearance without their trademark black-and-white makeup. The personas they created were never out of character when it came to their fans and the public-at-large.

What you wear on stage, what you say and how you say it during interviews and in public while representing your act should align with your brand's ideals and image. Answering interview questions and interacting with fans and music industry writers, reporters, bloggers, and so on, should be planned and rehearsed. It might sound like overkill and an awful lot of work, but it's needed to ensure consistency. With consistency comes fan loyalty. Many of those loyal fans will become evangelists for you and help spread the word much more than you and your group's members could do on your own.

POSITIONING

If your brand lives in the minds of your audience, positioning is the place where it lives in those minds.

Al Reis and Jack Trout introduced the concept of positioning in 1981. Here's their definition from their book *Positioning: The Battle for Your Mind*: "Positioning is an organized system for finding a window in the mind. It is based on the concept that communication can only take place at the right time and under the right circumstances."[5] Think of positioning as that place in your prospects' and clients' minds where your brand sets up housekeeping.

Positioning has a lot to do with differentiation—in other words, how you are different from all the other bands and acts out there. Granted, there are some bands whose entire act is all about copying some other band or solo performer. There are loads of Beatles tribute bands. The same goes for Pink Floyd and many other acts. I saw an ad the other day for a performer who impersonated Nat King Cole and another who cloned Madonna. But most artists want to develop their own sound and identity. That's where positioning comes in. As with your overall branding strategy, a positioning strategy begins with some questions. Here are a few to help get you started:

- What, if any, position do you currently own in the minds of your fans?

    This is, obviously, a good question for involving key fans and influencers with whom you have a relationship. You may find that the image and position you think you're projecting isn't what the audience is thinking.

- What position do you want to own?
- What are the obstacles you must overcome to reach that position?

    Overcoming obstacles can simply mean cleaning up your presentation so that it's consistent. It can also mean knocking out a competitor who occupies the position you want. That can be difficult, at best, when going toe-to-toe. A better approach might be redefining your position so you can occupy a spot that isn't already taken. For example, many years ago, Coca-Cola held the top spot when it came to soft drinks. 7-Up wanted that spot but simply couldn't compete against Coke. Coke's position was simply too deeply engrained in consumers' minds. In a brilliant twist, 7-Up entered the arena as the Uncola. They defined a completely new position that proved to be highly successful.

- Do you have the resources to overcome these obstacles?

    This often means money for promotion, but for bands with more savvy and smarts than money, it can mean tapping into key fans, influencers, street teams, and similar resources to help you reach your desired position. For example, a grassroots word-of-mouth campaign could be developed to get people talking about your band and what it's all about (your desired position) while building buzz and awareness.

Once you've established yourself and own a position, don't forget that it takes effort, work, and consistency to hold onto it. It's unwise to believe that you can rest and bask in the warmth of your foothold in the minds of your fans. No doubt, there will be another band or act—odds are, several—who want to kick you out and gain your position. Consider all the bands and solo performers who have been one-hit wonders. They may have reached their goal, but, because of lack of a sound work ethic, inspiration, bad deals, support, and resources to maintain their glory days, they simply faded away.

MARKETING YOUR BAND OR SOLO ACT

First off, let's be clear. Marketing is not evil. It's not selling your soul to "the man." It's not manipulating your fans. Well . . . OK . . . it sort of is, but in a good way. When you strip away all the baloney and jargon, marketing is simply finding out what people want and then finding a way to give it to them. That's not so bad, now, is it? In your case, it's learning what your fans want from music and how that aligns with what you love to do. Then, it's a matter of finding the best ways to tell them about it. Marketing and promotion are necessary if you ever hope to make it out of the garage, get known, and build a loyal fan base. Plus, with the right attitude, it can actually be a lot of fun along the way.

Marketing, when done right, is all about being authentic. It's being true to yourself, your music, and your fans. People can smell a load of bull a mile away. Aside from being on one side of the stage as a performer, you're just like your fans, or you should be. They can relate to your music, message, attitude, and so on. It's why they're fans. You're a fan of this band or that, right? What motivates you to see a show or buy a song? Why are you a fan? Marketing your music is often a matter of putting yourself in your fans' shoes. What motivates you to take action will often be the same for your audience.

When it comes to marketing, New York City–based drummer Brian Doherty said,

As a sole proprietor and freelance musician, marketing and promotion happen almost everywhere and practically all the time. It's important to connect the links in the chain and to view every situation and every person as a potential source of business. For instance, my mechanic once set up a meeting with me and another customer—a fellow musician—thinking that we could do business together. Who would've thought that an auto mechanic could provide such a connection? Another example: A fellow teacher at my [child's] elementary school and I became friendly over time. She knew of my past as a freelance drummer.

She and her husband even came to see me play *RENT* on Broadway one night. One day she opened up about her family and mentioned that her sister was a lawyer in the entertainment business. It turned out that her sister was indeed a lawyer and was Vice President of Sony Music International and was partners with icon Tommy Mattola. (Her name is Michelle Anthony. Both Tommy and Michelle have since left Sony.) Much later, Michelle was able to get my music to Sony's A&R department.

I have dozens of stories like this where I met people and musicians in one situation that later on recommended me for record dates, Broadway shows, tours, and more.

With all that said, I can bullet a few of my own guerilla marketing and promotion tactics:

- Let everyone know you're open for business and what it is that you do. Then stay alert.
- Recognize everyone as a potential link to a business connection.
- Maintain an interest in what your colleagues are doing and support them, even if it's an "attaboy" kind of thing.
- Tell the business community—flat out—*exactly* what you want to do, or what the goal for this CD, tour, or project is. Don't be coy or manipulative. Just don't be pushy about it, and remain humble.
- Use media by sending out press releases promoting your events and accomplishments.
- Identify your angle and make it interesting and, for God's sake, somehow make it *more than just about you*. In other words, explain how your supporters and patrons will benefit from your show, music, or project. Remember that the media are always looking for interesting and unique content.
- Be grateful and reward every recommendation with a sincere "thank you."

YOUR MARKETING/BRANDING PLAN

With that said, it's time for the next step—putting a workable marketing plan together that addresses your branding and positioning goals, action plans, competition and audience profile, and more. What follows is an outline for a typical plan that you can use to draft your own:

- Summary (highlights of your plan)
- Goals
- Primary goal
- Secondary goal(s)
- Branding goal(s)
- Positioning goal(s)
- Definition of the band identity
- Audience/fan profile
- Competition
- Products and services
- Original music
- Live shows
- Digital downloads
- Merchandise
- Licensing
- Action/promotion plans
- Print
- Flyers, posters, business cards, and so forth
- Street team materials for distribution
- Internet
- Website
- Blog/podcast
- Email marketing
- Discussion group participation
- Facebook, MySpace, Twitter, and other social media
- Pandora, Spotify, and other platforms
- Online networking opportunities

- Offline networking opportunities
- Public relations
- Develop industry contacts list(s)
- Media
- Labels
- Producers, managers, agents, and so on
- Press kit
- Press releases
- Interview procedures
- Live show development
- What will you do?
- Props/special equipment (if/as needed)
- Playing benefits to gain recognition
- Merchandise
- Live show sales
- Website sales
- Other outlets
- Budget
- Marketing calendar

KEEPING UP MOMENTUM

In wrapping up branding, marketing, and planning, try to put as many of your marketing activities on autopilot as possible. If you've planned well and work your plan, you'll get busy. The tough thing for any small business owner is maintaining marketing momentum when the business is at its busiest. Yet that's exactly when the business needs to keep things up to ensure that the firm stays busy. What often happens is that a small business owner, a musician for example, puts a plan into action and starts to see positive results. Gigs and projects roll in. The business owner, or musician, gets busy and begins to put marketing on the back burner. Then the projects are completed, and the business finds itself needing to start from the beginning because momentum was lost. Starting over from scratch and rebuilding a fan base, as well as media and industry contacts, takes a long time—that is, if they can be replicated at all. In the music business, as in other creative industries, you're only as good as your last gig, CD, performance, or song. When you've had an audience and loyal fan base, yet you fail to keep them engaged and interact with them on various levels, you lose credibility. Once that's gone, it's awfully tough to find it again.

In the service industry, which includes music, the sales curve, or the time it takes to convert a client from first contact into a paying client, can be six to eight months. Sometimes the curve is even longer. A lot longer. That's a long time to go without revenue. But, with proper planning and implementation, you'll stay busy for the long haul.

4

Your Band's Website

In today's world, a website is a must-have for any performer. That's pretty much a given. It's how you and, more important, your fans and others use it that's the key. Sure, there are plenty of third-party sites on the web where you can establish a presence, promote yourself and your act, sell tunes, and so on. Facebook and ReverbNation come to mind. But your own site gives you a very valuable asset—control. With your own site, you control the branding. You control the content. Plus, if you use it to sell songs and merchandise, you can keep most of the money.

When executed correctly, your site can become the hub, or center point, for your promotional and marketing efforts. From your site, fans can sign up for your e-newsletter, listen to and purchase your music, learn about upcoming shows, connect with you on Facebook, Twitter, MySpace, and other third-party sites, and more. That's pretty valuable stuff.

But, before you start reaping the benefits of a site, some questions are in order, as well as some careful planning. Having crystal-clear goals and an intimate knowledge of your audience go miles toward developing a killer site that engages its visitors and keeps those visitors, now fans, coming back.

DEVELOPING A KILLER WEBSITE

I'll be using the term *killer website*, several times throughout this chapter. A definition, therefore, is in order. And here's one for you:

A killer website is one that engages its visitors, gives them what they want, and does so in a transparent manner that doesn't require visitors to jump through several hoops. Plus, it's memorable, informative, and compelling to bookmark and forward to friends and associates.

Sound like a tall order? It is. What it means, simply, is paying close attention to the "do's" and also the "don'ts." Inasmuch as your site should be creative, it's not really the place to reinvent the wheel. There are tried and true tactics and techniques that have been proven to work. Consider the following:

- Keep the design, look, and feel clean and professional. Every element on your site should be there for a reason.
- Use intuitive, predictable navigation.

   Don't force visitors to learn a new type of navigation method to get around your site. Ideally, a visitor should be able to get what they want in no more than two clicks. One is better.
- The design shouldn't overshadow the content. It should complement it.
- Don't use banner ads unless you have a lot of traffic or sponsors and ads are a potential revenue source.
- Keep the content digestible.

   Web users tend to scan pages, rather than read them. Use lists when appropriate. Keep paragraphs short and text blocks narrow. There are few things worse than having to read a block of text that's the width of your entire monitor.
- Be consistent throughout the site in terms of the content tone and overall design.
- Avoid Flash if possible or use it sparingly.
- Don't use a splash page.

   Splash pages are intro pages to a site. Whereas they may have been nifty back in the 1990s, when nobody really knew what they were doing when it came to web design, they serve no purpose today and can hurt your SEO (search engine optimization).

- Give careful thought to keywords and phrases.

  Test potential keywords with a tool such as Google's Keyword Tool. You can find it at www.adword.google.com/select/KeywordToolExternal. It will provide a wealth of information, including how many searches were conducted for a particular word or phrase and alternate keywords you may not have considered.

PLANNING YOUR WEBSITE

Before starting to plan your site, some background might be in order for those who aren't familiar with how this whole web thing works under the hood. It's important to get a handle on things at the beginning so that you don't find yourself tripping over yourself down the road and needing to redo your work.

There are two accounts you'll need—a domain name account and a hosting account. A domain name account is your version of www.yourband.com. It can be purchased from several sources, including GoDaddy.com, Register.com, and NetworkSolutions.com. When the web was young, Network Solutions was the only source to buy a domain name, and people paid around $75 for one. Now domain names can be obtained for under $10.

Although domain names are significantly less expensive today, it's much more difficult to get the name you want. If you have a very unique band name, it might be easier, but be prepared to settle for an alternate.

Consider this: In December 2011 there were roughly 400 million websites on the Internet and billions of pages within those sites.[6] It becomes readily apparent that securing the domain name you want can be a tough act. Beyond this, the web spawned a new industry of domain name brokers. These companies buy huge blocks of domain names in the hopes of selling them to folks. Getting mixed up with these companies can be problematic, at best. Although you might be able to purchase a "just-right" name from GoDaddy for under $10, a broker might want to charge you several thousand dollars or more for the name you want.

So, go for the name you want, ideally your name or your band's name, but also create a list of alternatives, such as YourBandNameMusic.com or YourBandNameOnline.com.

The most intuitive extension for domain names is .com and also the one you should shoot for, but there are plenty of others including .net, .info, .org, and .mobi for mobile devices. Actually, there are more than 300 extensions available worldwide for various purposes. There's nothing inherently wrong with having an extension other than .com; it simply requires a bit more marketing and promotion effort to get the name out to your public. When guessing, people will try .com first and then, maybe, try some others. Getting .info or .net into their brains will require more effort on your part.

The other account you'll need is a hosting account. A host is the server where your site files live. *Server* is nothing more than a fancy name for a hard drive that's connected to the Internet. Like domain names, hosting tended to be much more expensive when the web was just getting started. Nobody really knew what this stuff was worth. As competition grew, as always, prices came down. Now you can purchase a hosting account for less than $50 per year or roughly $4 per month. This will often be a basic account, but it should provide ample features for most musicians. For example, I use Hands On Web Hosting's Ultralite package for my sites. I pay for it annually, and it's $48. For that, here's what I get:

- 5 GB of storage
- Unlimited bandwidth
- Unlimited email accounts
- Unlimited email autoresponders (automatic emails)
- Unlimited MySQL databases (important for blogs and e-commerce)
- Wordpress and several other blogging applications
- Numerous scripts, or programs, that do all sorts of things

There are many options when it comes to hosting companies. As mentioned, I use HandsOnWebHosting.com. Similar hosts include

HostGator.com, LunarPages.com, Bluehost.com, and many others. A quick Google search for "hosting companies," or "compare hosting companies," will return plenty of contenders. Also, ask around to learn what hosting companies your friends and colleagues are using for their sites. Two of the most important things you'll want to find out is how good and responsive each site's support team is and how much "up" time each server has. Up time refers to the amount of time the server is running keeping sites live. It's normal to have some down-time for maintenance, but too much is a problem.

PUTTING IT DOWN ON PAPER

After settling on a domain name and short-listing some hosting companies, it's time to start putting your plan down on paper. This is another important step. An amazing thing happens when plans are written down. Stuff tends to actually get done. A written website plan gives it life and also holds you accountable.

Begin your plan with your goals and objectives. Goals are broad-based intentions. They're what you're trying to accomplish with your site in terms of the big picture. Clear, well-defined goals will be the foundation of your plan and steer the rest of your activities. Objectives, on the other hand, are more like action plans. They usually have a date associated with them and are quantifiable—in other words, measurable. So, a goal might be "Develop a method of selling and distributing our music via the site." An objective might be "Integrate PayPal into the site as a payment method by June 30, 2012."

With your goals and objectives in hand, begin to determine what pages will be needed and what elements, assets, and resources will be needed to populate those pages. Will your recordings need to be converted to mp3s? How do you stand on images? Do you need to have current band or individual photos taken? What about writing? Are you or another band member comfortable doing that, or will you need to hire a writer? Gathering your materials together before you start building the site will help move things along in a timely manner and, if you use a web designer or developer, it can save you some dough.

A typical band or musician website contains the following pages:

- Homepage
- Events calendar
- Bio(s)
- Music samples
- Lyrics
- Discography
- Photos
- Merchandise/store
- Media/press page
- Blog
- Contact info

Your site may have all of these page or just some of them. You may find you need specific pages for various topics. You may not be sure how to order your pages within the navigation bar. This is where a site map comes in handy. A site map shows how the pages within your site relate to each other through links and navigation and, frankly, it doesn't need to be a high-level design effort. A legal pad or some index cards will do the trick. If you have some graphics software, so much the better. Draw out boxes that represent the pages in your site. Add some lines or arrows that show what links to what. If you choose the index card route, write the page names on the cards and then lay them out on a table. Move them around until you believe things are just right. Then, move it over to paper. For a site map example, visit www.neiltortorella.com/sitemap-example.pdf.

DO IT YOURSELF OR HIRE A DESIGNER

Now for the big question: Should you build the site yourself or should you hire a designer or developer? By the way, a designer generally handles just the front-end of the site design—the "look and feel," if you will. This normally is about the site page layout, fonts and typography, colors, and various other visual elements. A developer typically takes care of the backend functionality. These are things such as links, scripts that do this and that, navigation functions, contact forms, and a myriad of other programming functions. These two individuals often work together as a team, along with a writer, but there are also people who handle both aspects of site building.

There are loads of tools available on- and offline to help you build a site. You might be lucky and have a band member or friend who can help you out. Lots of musicians go that route. You might really luck out and have a family member . . . like your father . . . who's willing to push a pixel or two. That was the case with Eric Knight, a web-savvy musician and self-promotion virtuoso. "I have the good fortune that my father is a webmaster, and we are both computer nerds. So, he builds [the site] and then I maintain it," said Knight. Eric's site is very well executed and incorporates all the elements I've written about so far. It's clean and contemporary and provides all the information a fan or the media could want. Plus, Knight's site ties into ReverbNation for videos, lots of music samples, lyrics, and much more. It's a great example for independent musicians and bands to follow. His site can be found at www.ericknightonline.com.

Not all acts are so fortunate. Sure, you could probably muddle through the work, drink lots of coffee (which will eventually degrade into tequila or vodka, guaranteed), get incredibly frustrated, and invent a litany of colorful new curse words and phrases. If that sounds like you, you might be wise to invest in hiring a web designer and/or developer. Contracting out your site's design and development can make your life a lot easier so that you can concentrate on your music. But, be aware, a good designer or developer doesn't come too cheap. Suffice to say the good ones, as in so many professions, are not inexpensive.

If you decide to go it alone, there are a few things you'll need beyond mp3s of your tunes, some content, images, and perhaps some performance videos. First, you'll need at least a basic understanding of HTML and PHP, the languages of websites. Next, you'll also need some artistic ability if you want your site to stand out and engage your audience. Some marketing savvy is important, as is an understanding of search engine optimization. A great deal of information, best practices, tools, and techniques can readily be found with a few web searches.

Whether you choose to do it yourself or hire a professional, there's a common process for building a site. It may vary slightly from designer to designer, but the broad strokes are usually the same. A typical process for a web designer is as follows:

Phase 1: Research, Content Creation, and Design

- Do research (audience, competition, design, etc.)
- Gather assets (existing assets, stock and custom images, mp3s, etc.)
- Write content and make revisions
- Complete preliminary design and layout
- Make revisions
- Get approvals

Phase 2: Development

- Set up development site
- Do wireframe development and testing (a stripped-down version of the key pages)
- Create pages (using HTML, PHP, CSS, etc.)
- Do additional programming and database development, as needed

Phase 3: Testing and Proofing

- Check cross-browser compatibility (Firefox, Safari, Chrome, Explorer, etc.)
- Check cross-platform compatibility (Windows, Macintosh)

- Proofread
- Test and verify links
- Submit to search engines
- Launch

With your goals in hand, your content gathered, a site map, and the background research handled, the process moves to the design phase. If you have some artistic flair, you might start from scratch. A graphics program is imperative when designing your site. Many use Photoshop to lay out the pages; others prefer Fireworks. They're similar programs, each with its individual plusses and minuses. If you don't have Photoshop, and shelling out a load of dough to buy a copy isn't your idea of a good time, consider an open-source solution. Gimp is an open-source, or free, image editor that works much like Photoshop. Partner Gimp with Inkscape, another open-source application, and you're on your way. Inkscape is a vector-based drawing program, very similar to Adobe Illustrator. It's useful to create logos and various other graphics that will be incorporated into your site and other marketing and promotional materials for that matter.

Once you've settled on the design, it's time to start turning it into a website. Before you start coding, the design is normally sliced up into smaller images that are then stitched back together with HTML and CSS. CSS stands for "cascading style sheets." Style sheets define the look, or presentation, of a site. HTML defines the content and structure of the site.

Many hosting companies include some type of online HTML editor in their hosting packages, and there are several open-source ones available for download off the web. PageBreeze, CoffeeCup, and Amaya are some examples. These are WYSIWYG editors, or "what you see is what you get." This type of visual editor makes the process much easier and lightens the amount of HTML you'll need to know. But knowing HTML is still a good idea when troubleshooting time rolls around.

If hiring a freelancer web designer or firm makes more sense for your situation and pocketbook, the designer often brings some valuable insights. First and foremost is that the designer is not you. The designer is not a band member. Heck, the designer may not even be a fan. That means the designer's viewpoint is more objective because he or she is not as close to things. Plus, the designer know the ropes when it comes to not only web design but also the background research, SEO, and tools and techniques to get the most out of your site. Well, providing, of course, that the designer is good at what he or she does.

Joe Deninzon of the band Stratospheerius hired a pro for the band's website. He said, "I hired a professional web designer. We live in the DIY age, but I'd rather hire someone who knows what they're doing to do my website and go write a new song in the meantime."

Hiring out the site building can be the best decision you can make . . . or the worst. Here's why: In many ways, working with a website designer, when you don't know much about building websites, is like working with an auto mechanic when you don't know much about the inner workings of the internal combustion engine. That nagging voice in the back of your head keeps repeating, "Is this person taking advantage of me?"

Most web designers are very ethical people who want nothing more than to build a brilliant site for your band. Sure, they want to get paid, too, but they are above board and not interested in taking you for a ride. However, there are some out there who will prey on your lack of knowledge.

Here are a few rules of thumb to keep you safe:

- Ensure your domain name and hosting accounts are in your name, not the designer's.

  You can run into trouble if your designer gets mowed over by a Mack truck or there's a falling out between the two of you. If I had a dime for every time I've heard this sort of story, and had to subsequently work things out so my client could have the site back, I'd be in the tropics sipping umbrella-laden drinks on the beach. Oh, wait. I live in the tropics. Nonetheless, the advice still stands.

- Create a request for proposal (RFP) that describes your goals, needs, deadlines, budget, timeline, and so forth.
- Get at least three estimates/proposals.
- Ensure that everything is "apples to apples."

    Don't be taken in by folks who want to up-sell you or give you something other than what you asked for. Put together a site project brief that describes the key elements, must-haves, and so on. Think of a project brief as though it were a set list for your next gig. With a set list, the whole band plays the same songs at the same time. You avoid the bassist playing "Purple Haze," while the singer's crooning out "Crazy Train."

- Have a project agreement/contract.
- Reduce costs by providing as much content, assets (graphics, images, etc.) as possible.
- If possible, include audience/fan research.
- Provide content digitally whenever possible.
- Keep on top of progress, but don't micromanage.

The more material and information you can provide to your designer, the less time the designer will have to invest into the site, and that means a lower cost, in most cases. One other word to the wise: If you don't understand something, ask. Many designers and developers get hung up with trade jargon—all those technical terms and alphabet soup such as ASP, PHP, FTP, Javascript, and so on. The designer probably isn't trying to confuse you. Designers just use these terms all the time and tend to forget that they can make a layperson's head hurt.

If at all possible, have a content management system (CMS) included in your site. A CMS is a backend tool that will allow you to maintain the site with relative ease once it's live. There are several open-source options when it comes to CMS, and your designer may have one that he or she uses often.

Many are turning to Wordpress as a CMS, and that's what drummer-for-hire Brian Doherty did. He said, "At first I had a pro do it [the website] and then realized that in order to update the content, I'd have to learn to do it. Thus, I use Blogger and Wordpress—free and easy."

Originally a blogging application (which it still is), Wordpress has become very popular for building and managing complete websites. It's free and relatively easy to use, but it can also be extremely robust. Wordpress utilizes "plug-ins," or small applications, often free, that perform all sorts of functions. There are plug-ins to handle contact forms, SEO, image galleries, and much more. For musicians, there are Wordpress plug-ins that tie into ReverbNation and SoundCloud, create performance calendars, stream music, integrate social media, and more. Plus, given its blogging roots, with Wordpress, a blog can be easily created and incorporated into your site.

Similar to Wordpress, Drupal and Joomla are popular options for building an easy-to-maintain site. Singer-songwriter Anna Fermin took the Drupal route with her partner:

> My collaborator/business partner, Aaron Barber, took on the building of our website. It was built using Drupal, which Aaron learned on his own from the bottom up. Because my other talents lie in graphic design, we were able to team up to build and design our site. It was a lot of work and time put in for Aaron to learn the language of Drupal, but we had a very small budget, and, for what we wanted, we were going to need to implement on our own. We simply couldn't afford to hire someone to do it for us. In the end, we got exactly what we wanted: a website with a highly customized look and functionality. No cookie-cutter website here.

KEEPING IN TOUCH WITH FANS VIA AN E-NEWSLETTER

Savvy musicians know that they need to continually market and promote themselves to stay on their fans' radar screens. They've learned that marketing isn't evil. Marketing is their best bet to slay the monster called "feast or famine syndrome." Keeping the lines of communication open between you and your fans is imperative to building your fan base, as well as selling tickets, music, and merchandise. Finding tools that work and keep a musician top-of-mind is critical to help ensure future gigs and sales. So, finding the right tools—tools that are both inexpensive and work—is pretty darn important.

Fortunately, we live in a day and age where there are loads of online marketing and promotion tools and tactics that won't break the bank. Many are even free. The web has radically changed the way musicians, and businesses in general, leverage and implement their marketing efforts. Gone are the days of promoting a show with posters tacked to telephone poles.

Enter the old standby, email marketing, and its younger cousin, social media. Facebook, with its 900+ million users, is free, as is Twitter. A blog or podcast can be great tools for a musician to share thoughts, present music, sell tickets, and feature merchandise. YouTube also offers an excellent platform for getting the word out with video.

But there's some talk out there that email marketing is becoming a thing of the past, what with all this social media and networking stuff going on. I beg to differ. I believe it's still a very viable marketing tool. Here's why:

- E-newsletters are dirt-cheap to produce.
- Email marketing has one of the highest returns on investment (ROI) indexes of all marketing channels. In fact, it is the highest
- Response cycles for email are pretty darn quick.
- Email is an effective and an oh-so-handy way of driving people to your website, blog, and social media outlets such as your band's Facebook page.
- Email is highly trackable.

    You can track who opened your email, when they opened it, what links were clicked, and more. That's great to learn what's important to your audience.

- Emails are forwardable.

  When was the last time you received a marketing piece by snail mail and were so taken by it that you slapped a label and stamp on it and mailed it to a friend?

A recent DMA study showed email marketing's average ROI to be an astounding $40.56 for every dollar spent. That's more than double Internet marketing's ROI of $19.94 for every dollar spent on banner ads and such.[7] That fact alone should motivate you to get into email marketing, if you haven't done so already.

Like followers on Twitter and other social media outlets, email subscribers have expressed an interest in what you have to say. They've "opted in" by subscribing or following you. This is called inbound, or permission, marketing, where the fans find you. Outbound marketing involves what most people would call traditional marketing and advertising techniques. It includes print and broadcast ads, posters, flyers, direct mail, and so on. The thing all these methods have in common is that the business finds the prospects and interrupts them with a marketing message the prospects probably don't want to hear or see. So, they tune it out. It seems to me that having a list of 500 prospects and influencers who have said they want to hear from you is significantly better than a list of, say, 10,000 who will probably never see your show or buy a tune or T-shirt.

Outbound marketing is a numbers game. More impressions equals more sales. An impression happens each time the audience sees or hears your message. It's a shotgun approach that's bloated with waste. For example, the average response rate for direct mail ranges from around 0.5 percent to 2 percent.[8] Getting a 2-percent response is considered to be pretty darn good and has the advertiser doing the happy dance.

But let's flip that over for a minute. A 2-percent response rate means that 98 percent was wasted. In effect, the marketer, or musician in this case, is throwing away an awful lot of hard-earned money while thinking he or she is doing good. It simply doesn't add up or make any kind of fiscal sense. Well, it makes perfect sense to whoever is selling direct mail programs.

Alas, I digress. So, is email marketing dead? I don't think so. It has, however, changed its role. In the beginning, email marketing was an independent act. Nowadays, it needs to be a team player. Email marketing and social media should be two elements of an overall promotion plan and program for musicians. Each element within the program should promote the other with a value-packed, consistent voice.

Want more hard truth? Here you go: Crafting your message with quality information that's authentically useful to your fans is paramount. Why? Because fans ultimately want to know what's in it for them. Where's the payoff? Be sure to give them one with each message, and they'll keep coming back for more. In a nutshell, your e-marketing efforts and your entire marketing program should be all about the audience and not about you. Promote your tour dates, but also give people some sound bytes, if not full songs. Have a contest and give away a few T-shirts or other merchandise. Give your subscribers a reason to open your messages each time they hit the inbox.

GETTING READY FOR EMAIL MARKETING

It's not practical to send out an e-newsletter from your computer's email application such as Outlook or Mac Mail. The main reason is that your Internet service provider (ISP) or hosting company might close your account or suspend it if you send more than 100 emails at a time. Sending too many messages is a big red flag that you might be a spammer. One hundred is a fairly typical cap that sets off an automatic server response by the ISP or host. These companies need to protect themselves and their customers.

Another reason is that there's no way to track your message and analyze the results. Without some tracking method and analytics in place, you're emailing in the dark, never knowing if your messages are effective, or even being opened for that matter.

Fortunately, there are several email marketing services available to help you out. Constant Contact, Vertical Response, MailChimp, AWeber, and iContact are just a few. While each has its specialty and focus, they all typically offer templates, manage the opt-in and -out process, manage subscriber lists, provide sign-up box code for your site, and offer a wealth of email marketing information.

With regard to specialties, for example, Constant Contact, a very popular service, focuses on integrating emails with events. Let's say you have a show coming up. Constant Contact lets you set up an event information page that includes a description of the show and its time and location, along with a map. Plus, these information pages are highly customizable. You can add links to your site, to social media, and even to sound bytes and video. You can also add links to purchase tickets, merchandise, and more.

The information page is tied to an email message that is sent to your subscriber list on a predetermined day and time. You can also set up multiple email messages to be sent at predetermined times on specific dates. After the message is sent, you can log onto your Constant Contact account and review the message statistics. This is very handy stuff. You can see how many subscribers, by name, opened your email, when they opened it, how many times they opened it, what links they clicked, how many opt-outs were requested, and how many email addresses bounced. These statistics, over time, allow you to learn what's important to your subscribers and to develop content that is valuable to them, based on open rates and click throughs.

AWeber offers similar features and tools but focuses on autoresponders. An autoresponder is an automatic email, or series of emails, that is sent after a trigger is activated, usually subscribing to an e-newsletter or responding to a free download offer, often some sort of e-book or report. It can be a great way to keep in touch with your subscribers without needing to craft emails all the time. You create the response, or responses, once, set up the sending schedule, and you're done. Autoresponders can be useful to promote a new CD or single-song downloads, upcoming shows, news, and other information.

But what about developing content for regular e-newsletters? That can become a challenge for many small business owners in a fairly short time. Here are some ideas:

- Upcoming shows
- Band or musician news
- New music
- New merchandise
- Band member profiles
- Song backgrounds—how and why you wrote a particular tune
- Links to YouTube video clips
- Requests for performance and song feedback
- New blog posts
- Social media highlights

Social media can be a great thing and will be discussed in depth in the next chapter. But social media posts, tweets, and the like tend to get lost in the shuffle. These outlets go by rather fast, and everybody is in a frantic pace to be heard. Email marketing isn't as rushed. Your subscribers are subscribers because they want to hear from you. That's golden. Odds are, these fans will take the time to open your messages and follow a few links. In return, give them something beyond news. Consider giving away a couple of T-shirts or other merchandise, just for your subscribers. Maybe you could hold a contest and offer a backstage pass with a "meet and greet" the band for the winner. People want to feel special, and they want to be part of a group. An offer such as "Just for our newsletter subscribers . . ." can be a great motivator and also encourage your subscribers to pass on your newsletter signup information to their friends.

With your email marketing in place, it's a good idea to have at least three or four newsletters written and ready to go. As your marketing and promotion efforts begin to pay off, you'll get busy. When you get busy, you'll forget to get your newsletter ready to go. So, you miss a month. Then two. The next thing you know, your subscribers are opting out, and your newsletter fizzles away. Having a few newsletters in place and scheduled to be published will help ensure that doesn't happen and you don't find yourself in a scramble to send out something. When you're rushed, errors happen and your newsletter efforts tend to become weak.

A WORD ABOUT SELLING MERCHANDISE ONLINE

Selling merchandise, such as T-shirts, hats, mugs, posters, and similar items, can be a nice shot in the revenue arm for solo performers and bands. But there's still a notion that selling stuff online is an easy road to riches. It's not. Getting even a loyal fan to dig into their pocket and pull out some cash or a credit card is no easy task. But it can be done.

Before you can sell stuff, you'll need some stuff to sell. Sure, that's a no-brainer, but it's not as simple as it may sound. You have some options. If you want to sell T-shirts, for example, the conventional route is to hire a designer to create the design, or do it yourself. With art in hand, it's off to the silk screener, where you'll need to buy shirts and pay the printer. Then, you'll need to store the finished shirts somewhere, arrange for a payment method, whether it be cash, checks, credit cards, or, ideally, a combination of those options. You'll also need to make shipping arrangements for sales that aren't local to you. You'll need to have some sort of return policy, in most cases. That's an awful lot of time, money, and effort to sell some shirts. In fact, it can quickly turn into its own full-time business.

Here's a better idea: Let the Internet come to the rescue. There are several sites where you can create all sorts of products and have them created and fulfilled on demand. That means you won't need to carry an inventory. You sell one shirt. They print and ship one shirt.

The grand daddy of these services is CafePress.com, which is the seasoned pro when it comes to web-based on-demand printers. A Cafe-Press account is free to set up. Free is good. They offer a wide range of products, including apparel, drink ware, posters, key chains, tote bags, and more, right down to license plate frames, all of which you can slap your logo and site address on.

Add your CafePress store link to your site, e-newsletter, and other outlets, such as Facebook and MySpace pages, Twitter, and so forth. When someone buys a product, the magic starts. CafePress receives the order, prints up the product, and handles the shipping for you. Plus, the company offers several promotional tools and information resources, including customizable widgets for your site. CafePress makes it easy and is a fairly risk-free method to sell merchandise online.

Selling merchandise is only one part of the story. When fans buy your merchandise, it becomes a promotional tool. In effect, your fans are paying you for the privilege of promoting your act. When a fan wears one of your shirts or hats, think about how many others will see it and maybe visit your site or ask about your music.

In closing out this chapter, your website and your e-newsletter or email marketing plan are, arguably, the most important elements in your overall marketing and promotion efforts. Don't leave them to chance. Give each the quality thought and planning it demands to be effective. With a little savvy, both can be implemented without a lot of cash, and the return can far outweigh the investment.

5

The Importance of Social Media for Musicians

Social media is a phenomenon. In a relatively short amount of time, it has changed the way we humans communicate. It's gone from a medium of telling folks what you're having for lunch to a marketing powerhouse that companies leverage to get the word out to their audience, soliciting followers and "likes" in an effort to forge relationships and ultimately sell more products and services. Musicians are also using it to build relationships with fans, get the word out about upcoming shows, spread news, and sell their music. Considering that I like Jimi Hendrix's and Janis Joplin's Facebook pages, it seems as though social media even reaches beyond the grave. Now that's some powerful stuff.

In this chapter, I'll explore the various social media outlets and some of the best practices you can implement to get the most mileage for your time investment. Yup, I wrote "time investment." Allow me to explain. I do a social media presentation for small businesses. Actually, at three-plus hours, it's more of a workshop. Inevitably, about halfway through the presentation, someone will raise their hand and ask, "This is all great, but doesn't it take an awful lot of time?" In a word, yes. Like most things, what you put into it is proportionate to what you get out of it. But, if not managed correctly, you can easily find yourself putting in a lot of time with little, if anything, to show for your efforts.

FACEBOOK

If you're like almost 1 billion other people on Planet Earth, at the time of this writing, you've got a Facebook profile. It's your personal profile page where you bring your friends up to speed about what you're doing, comment on what they're doing, and share the occasional link, article, viral video, and funny image. What you may not have is a Facebook *page* dedicated to your music, band, or act. If you don't, you should get one . . . now. Facebook has three levels of user interaction: (1) People have profiles; (2) organizations, causes, and like-minded folks can also have groups; and (3) businesses, including musicians, have pages. The reality is that just due to its sheer user numbers, Facebook can't be ignored. Let's look at those numbers, courtesy of HowManyAreThere. org:

- 901 million monthly active users at the end of March 2012
- Approximately 80 percent of monthly active users outside the United States and Canada
- 526 million daily active users on average in March 2012
- 488 million monthly active users who used Facebook mobile products in March 2012, and more than 500 million mobile monthly active users as of April 20, 2012
- An average of 398 million users active on at least six out of the last seven days during March 2012
- More than 125 billion friend connections at the end of March 2012
- An average of 3.2 billion likes and comments generated by users per day during the first quarter of 2012
- More than 42 million pages with ten or more likes at the end of March 2012
- Availability in more than 70 languages[9]

Those are pretty impressive statistics and a testament to why you or your band needs to have a Facebook presence, and a robust one, at that. Facebook provides a medium to reach out to your fans not only on their desktop or laptop computers but also on their mobile devices, which is a fast-growing segment of the audience and the web-at-large for that matter.

Begin by pointing your browser to www.facebook.com/pages/create.php, where you can select "Artist, Band, or Public Figure." Next, choose a category—in your case, "Musician or Band." Pop in your name or the name of your band and agree to Facebook's terms.

Once your page is created, it's time to start dressing it up. Early in 2012, Facebook changed the layout for personal profiles and pages, adding in the "timeline" and "cover image." The cover image appears at the top of a Facebook page, is 851 pixels by 315 pixels, and ideally is less than 100 KB. It can be pretty much anything you like except a blatant sales message. Do some Facebook searches for musicians and bands you like, and you'll get a good idea of what is being done. As mentioned, if you haven't shelled out a ton of money for Photoshop, open-source image editor Gimp has you covered for creating your cover image.

After uploading your cover image, complete the "About" page, giving your fans the lowdown on who you are, what your music is about, how your act developed, and similar information. Be sure to include your contact information so that all those booking agents can get in touch.

Use the "Photos" section to upload performance images, band member photos, and related pictures. Populate the "Events" section with upcoming show dates and other events. You might consider using the "Notes" section to write your thoughts about shows, music you're writing or recording, and such. Tapping into the Networked Blogs app can bring your blog posts into Facebook. That's handy to help build your blog's readership.

One of the most important aspects of a Facebook Page is to make it personal. You want to not only reach out to your fans but also have them reach out to you and feel as though they know you personally. Sure, you'll post updates about your music, but also post items that are of interest to you beyond music. Doing so can go a long way toward cementing those fan relationships.

Use your Facebook page to give your fans a backstage pass of sorts. One of the great features of Facebook is its mobile connectivity. As you're getting ready to play a show, send a few updates from your phone to your page about what you're doing to prepare for the performance, how excited you and your band mates feel about playing the venue, and what's happening backstage. This gives your fans, many of whom are probably in the audience, some insight into you and the show, but it also lifts the curtain, so to speak, and brings you closer to your fans. It's a simple thing, but it can be very effective.

Reach out to other bands, performers, and music industry folks via Facebook. These can be bands and artists you've worked or performed with along the way or just acts that you admire, where you're the fan. This is a great way to help increase the number of page "likes."

Don't forget to use the various third-party apps that are available for use with your Facebook page. BandPage, ReverbNation, and Damn-theradio bring in elements such as music players, events listings, merchandise sales tools, "like" gates, and email list builders. (*Like gating*, by the way, is forcing a Facebook user who has not already liked your page to like it before they can see content on a particular custom Facebook tab.)

Finally, remember that it's not all about you. Engage your fans by asking their opinions, posing questions, and making them feel special. Get them involved. As mentioned in the previous chapter, people want to feel that they're special and part of a group. So, as with email marketing, create special offers, deals, and exclusive Facebook content.

TWITTER

Having a Facebook page is a good start, but there's still much to do. Twitter is your next step. Like Facebook, it can't be ignored if for no other reason than sheer numbers. Your fans are on Twitter, and you need to meet them on their turf.

Before you start tweeting, give consideration to how your band or personal brand should be perceived. If you're a solo performer, that's pretty straightforward. If you have a band, will you tweet under the band's name, or will the individual members manage their own accounts?

As mentioned, domain names are becoming tougher to secure. It's the same with Twitter. Be prepared to settle for something that's perhaps less than ideal. For example, solo musician Eric Knight, who has a reasonably common name, uses eric_knight. Similarly, Tower of Power uses TOP; I don't know if that's by design or not, but TowerofPower is owned by someone else.

Twitter has a name search function that will simply tell you if the handle you type in when you set up your account is already taken. You might also try other services such as Tweexchange.com. Namechk. com is something of a one-stop shopping site for available names on numerous sites.

When you consider your branding, give careful thought to your profile information and your background image. For example, Paul McCartney uses a simple black background with his signature in white. He can do that because . . . well . . . he's Paul McCartney, after all. Many artists use a performance image, while others use their logo. The point is to be creative and reinforce your brand.

From a design production standpoint, Twitter backgrounds are aligned to the left. That's where your important information should go. These are things like your act's name/logo, contact information, website address, and so forth. For 99 percent of your visitors, a left-side width of 66 pixels is safe. The overall size of my Twitter background (left to right) is 1600 pixels with a height of 1200 pixels. It seems to work well for my followers and visitors, because most have larger screens. The key is to nail your core design and then test it in various sizes on different resolution monitors. Something that looks great on a 24-inch monitor may be covered up by tweet content on a 15-inch monitor.

Some fans favor Facebook. Others like Twitter. Yet others are into various other social media outlets. That means duplicating your communications. Actually, "duplicating" probably isn't the best word. "Similar" is likely better. Communications should provide the necessary information but also be targeted to the particular audience. Twitter gives you

140 characters to get your message in front of fans. You can say much more on Facebook. Play to the strengths of each medium and be sure to cross-promote. Tweet about what's happening on your Facebook page and vice versa.

Tweets should carry upcoming performance dates and locations, the occasional merchandise offer specifically for your followers, and conversations with your fans and others in the music industry. It's also a good idea to get a bit personal. What are you working on in terms of songs or CDs? What are the band members up to? How did a performance go? Links to helpful information about technique, equipment, and such are often overlooked but can be very valuable to your fans who are also musicians.

Here's a little story about the power of Twitter. Although he's a graphic designer and not a musician (nobody's perfect), my friend, Calvin Lee, is a Twitter master. Here's his story.

> I started back in June of 2008. I heard a buzz about Twitter from my friends, how cool it was. I finally gave it a try. Initially, I didn't really like it at all. I didn't want to know what *you* were doing, like shopping or watching a TV program. A couple of weeks into it, I stopped using Twitter. It wasn't for me.
>
> Months later, I felt the pressure from my friends to give Twitter another shot. I tried another strategy. I started following designers. I retweeted their articles, shared information, and tried to be helpful. That did it! I was hooked since then.

Since that time, Cal has become a major influencer on Twitter with a following of just under 80,000 at the time of this writing. No doubt he'll be closing in on 100,000 by the time you read this. He's seen as a celebrity in many circles. He added, "Twitter and social media really gets your name out there. The results of social media ha[ve] gotten me everything from recognition at conferences to VIP treatment, complimentary products and services, round trip airline tickets, hotel suites, and movie tickets, to name a few. "It's gotten me more work and PR than all of the other traditional ways of promoting yourself, such as advertising. Twitter is a combination of word of mouth [and] building relationships and trust all at once."

The amazing thing about Cal is that he found success without the aid of any Twitter automation tools. There are several tools to automate and schedule tweets. Many integrate with other social media as well. I confess: I'm guilty of this. I use HootSuite. It lets me set up my tweets with link shortening, if needed, to keep within the 140-character limit. I can write one tweet and then shoot it out to Facebook, LinkedIn, RSS, and various other outlets. Handy? You bet. But it's a bad idea to automate everything. You start sounding robotic. That might be fine for Styx's "Mr. Roboto," but not you. It's best to use the automation tools but also intermingle live tweets, links, discussions, and so on. This way you still come off as being human and personal.

In the end, Twitter is one of those things you simply need to play around with to see what works for you and, more important, your followers.

YOUTUBE

As you probably know, YouTube is an outlet to share videos. What you might not know it that it's also the most searched site next to its parent company, Google. From YouTube's site: "Founded in February 2005, YouTube allows billions of people to discover, watch and share originally created videos. YouTube provides a forum for people to connect, inform, and inspire others across the globe and acts as a distribution platform for original content creators and advertisers large and small."

For artists, YouTube provides an outlet and distribution method to share performance videos, instructional bits, interviews, and more. And if you've got something really good, it might just go viral (another word for everybody in the world watching your stuff).

First, set up an account for your act. Then brand it. These are called "channels." You'll find a link to set up your account under your name or avatar in the upper right corner of the site.

Creating a YouTube channel lets you upload videos, create playlists, and respond to videos with comments and control how comments are handled (shown or hidden). Within your settings, you can also create a custom username. So, if one band member, manager, or publicist handles this for you, a custom username is a handy thing to identify your act. It's also important to note that YouTube pulls in much information from your Google account. So, if you don't have one of those, it would be a good idea to get one. It's easy.

Channel branding is a great idea to tie your brand together. YouTube offers many options for this, including a custom header (970 pixels wide and up to 150 high), custom colors, and custom backgrounds. Background images can be up to 1 MB, but something in the area of 256 KB is better when it comes to page loading times. You don't want your visitors to have to hang around waiting for your background to load, because they won't. They'll leave to watch something else . . . like a competitive act's videos.

Another good thing about YouTube videos is that you can embed them into your site, blog, and Facebook page. That means you'll be tapping YouTube's bandwidth, not yours. That becomes important when you start to become popular. When site visitors click on your video, that requires a thing called bandwidth. It's akin to a pipe that carries your data back and forth. It also costs money. You'll get a reasonable amount included within your hosting package. But if you go over the allotted amount, your site will, in most cases, automatically shut down and display the notorious "bandwidth exceeded" screen. That would be bad. Avoid this altogether by hosting your videos on YouTube and then linking to the site or, better, using the YouTube "embed" code that's found by clicking "Share" under a video on the site.

When it comes to actually shooting videos, a smartphone is great . . . for your fans. You should try to do better. Have a pro, or at least a friend with a decent camcorder, record your performances. The quality will be much better, and so will the sound. Don't play around with this. Quality counts. How many concert videos have you seen that utterly sucked? Don't be one of them.

PODCASTS

A podcast is really nothing more than an Internet radio show. It might be talk, discussion, training, or music (which is good for you). Podcasts can be attached to your site, blog, RSS feed, or, for our purposes, iTunes. Why? It's a fairly easy inroad into the iTunes world, a place you want to be seen or, in this case, heard.

Podcasts can be a do-it-yourself task or handled by a third party. Because you're likely on a budget, the DIY route is probably best. The first thing you'll need is a recording application. You may already have one if you're one of the lucky acts with the dough to buy one. If you're not, no worries. There's an open-source application (there's always one, isn't there?) called Audacity. It can be found at http://audacity.sourceforge.net/download/ and is available for Windows, Mac (recommended), and, for the rebel in you, Linux. Version 2.0 is the most current at the time of this writing and offers several new and improved features, including the following:

- Many effects significantly improved, especially Equalization, Noise Removal, and Normalize. Vocal Remover now included plus GVerb on Windows and Mac. VAMP analysis plug-ins now supported.
- Improved label tracks with Sync-Lock Tracks feature in the Tracks Menu. Multiple clips per track. Tracks and selections can be fully manipulated using the keyboard. Many more keyboard shortcuts.
- New Device Toolbar to manage inputs and outputs. Timer Record feature. New Mixer Board view with per-track VU meters.
- Automatic Crash Recovery in the event of abnormal program termination.
- Fast "On-Demand" import of WAV/AIFF files if read directly from source. FLAC now fully supported. Added support for optional FFmpeg library for import/export of AC3/M4A/WMA and import of audio from video files.

Audacity allows for multi-tracking, mixing, and much, much more. It's more than enough to record your podcast, or even demos, for that matter. One important point: Invest in a quality microphone. It will really help. Also, to export mp3s, you may need to download an application called the LAME MP3 encoder. It's not really lame and actually does a great job of converting native Audacity files into mp3s. It can be found at http://lame1.buanzo.com.ar/. It's free, but I'm sure the creators would appreciate a donation, if you feel so inclined.

Once you have your killer cast, you'll want to get it out to the world to be heard. This is where iTunes comes in. You'll need to create an RSS feed for your podcast and jump through a few hoops in the beginning. After that, it gets a lot easier. For information about how to set up your podcast, visit www.apple.com/itunes/podcasts/specs.htmlCached - Similar

REVERBNATION

ReverbNation is a great site and tool for musicians. It was started by five partners: Michael Doernberg, CEO; Lou Plaia, VP, Artist Development; Jed Carlson, Chief Marketing Officer; Robert Hubbard, Chief Technology Officer; and Steve Jernigan, VP of Partner Integration. The concept for ReverbNation was developed in 2005, and the company was founded in 2006.

According to their site, ReverbNation is home to over 2.35 million musicians, venues, labels, and industry professionals. In other words, it's the place to be, be heard, and be found. From their site: "ReverbNation provides over 2.35 million music industry professionals—artists, managers, labels, venues, festivals/events—with powerful, easy-to-use technology to promote and prosper online. Our wide array of distribution and promotional solutions provides the hands-on tools and actionable insights that allow musicians and industry professionals to reach their goals in an increasingly complex music world. We operate worldwide with customers on every continent. In fact, over 30 million visitors come to reverbnation.com every month. And of course, we Love Music!"

The site offers musicians a fairly full set of music management features, including the following:

- Full-featured profiles, including a ReverbNation profile, Facebook integration, and a website building tool with numerous promotional functions
- Fan Management, which allows you to import email and social media lists and send and manage fan communications, such as e-newsletters and fan collection widgets
- Enhanced Facebook promotion
- Reverb Store
- Distribution via iTunes and more
- Gig finder
- Your own mobile app
- And more

While the majority of ReverbNation features and services are free, they do offer expanded services with a paid subscription. At the time of this writing, their Complete Package, designed for emerging artists, is just $16.67, billed annually. Not a bad deal for all you get.

MYSPACE

With the powerful emergence and presence of Facebook, MySpace seems to have gone by the wayside. And it did in many ways. But the word on the street is that it's redefining itself to again become the musical Mecca it once was.

From MySpace's site:

Myspace LLC is a leading social entertainment destination powered by the passions of fans. Aimed at a Gen Y audience, Myspace drives social interaction by providing a highly personalized experience around entertainment and connecting people to the music, celebrities, TV, movies, and games that they love. These entertainment experiences are available through multiple platforms, including online, mobile devices, and offline events.

Myspace is also the home of Myspace Music, which offers an ever-growing catalog of freely streamable audio and video content to users and provides major, independent, and unsigned artists alike with the tools to reach new audiences. The company is headquartered in Beverly Hills, CA, and is a subsidiary of Specific Media.

Although it is not as feature-rich as ReverbNation, nor is it really designed to be, MySpace provides yet another platform to be heard. The service features "what's trending," playlists, movies, and various other entertainment-related information. It's still where your act should have a presence and also a site to definitely keep an eye on as its re-branding and upgrades continue.

SOCIAL MEDIA TOOLS FOR ARTISTS

As mentioned earlier, there are several automation and other tools to enhance and expedite your social media presence. Some of these include the following:

- HootSuite.com
  HootSuite is a tool that allows you to manage several social media accounts and post to them at scheduled times. It will also provide link shortening and analytics for your tweeting efforts.
- SocialOomph.com
  Similar to HootSuite, Social Oomph also allow scheduling of posts, tracking of tweets, unlimited accounts, auto-following and auto direct messages to new followers, Facebook integration, scheduling and publishing of blog posts, and much more.

- ReverbNation's My Band for Facebook
  This tool allows for band photo additions and streaming songs and performances.
- Twiturm
  Twiturm allows you to tweet your music without sending a fan to a third-party site such as MySpace.
- FanBridge
  FanBridge lets you keep in touch with fans via e-newsletters and other communication media through one handy source.
- BandCamp
  BandCamp is a do-it-yourself digital music distribution solution. In effect, it lets you build, produce, and distribute your music, complete with lyrics and artwork, at a fairly reasonable price. It will also track statistics. Plus, you still own everything, and that's a huge plus.
- Band Metrics
  All this stuff is for naught if you can't learn how and what's working. Band Metrics lets you do that. No more guessing. Now you can know what's doing the job, selling the tunes, and bringing in the fans.

SOCIAL MEDIA WRAP-UP

When all is said and done, social media is an indie artist's best friend. Tools are free or dirt-cheap. The fans are there, waiting to hear from you. Sure, it's a time investment, but it sure beats paying through the nose for a PR firm or high-priced publicist who's probably more interested in the fee or commission than your success.

Take the time to think and develop a sound strategy of what you're trying to accomplish. Don't try to be all things to all people. Play to your strengths, and play to your fans' wants and needs. Communicate with your fans regularly. Be human. Don't be an ass. Provide good-quality content, and the fans will beat a path to your venue doors. They might even buy a T-shirt or CD, too.

6

The Future Is Now:
New Opportunities for
Collaboration, Promotion,
Distribution, and More

Is the album dead? More aptly put, "Are the vinyl album and CD dead?" Full albums don't seem to fit in well with the current direction of the music industry. Sure, the labels would love to keep them going, but the masses seem to be more interested in downloading a single tune while forgetting the other tracks. This is a tough pill to swallow for many artists who put in long, laborious hours honing songs that fit together like a well-made glove.

Consider the concept album. You know . . . albums such as The Beatles' *Sgt. Pepper's Lonely Hearts Club Band*, Pink Floyd's *The Wall*, Queen's *Songs for the Deaf*, The Beach Boys' *Pet Sounds*, Jethro Tull's *Thick as a Brick*, David Bowie's classic *The Rise and Fall of Ziggy Stardust and the Spiders from Mars*—and who could forget *Tommy* by The Who, which is technically a rock opera. The list goes on and on. These were albums that depended on each song to build the next. They told a story.

Some definitions and a brief history lesson are in order again. A concept album is an album that is held together by a unified theme. It might be musical, lyrical, or otherwise. The thing is, the album is tied together and creates a message for the listener. A non-concept, or typical, album is a collection of unrelated songs, even though they may be great individually. The first accepted concept album was Woody Guthrie's *Dust Bowl Ballads* (released in 1940). *Songs of Our Soil* and *Ride This Train* (released in 1959 and 1969, respectively) by Johnny Cash were also considered concept albums. Jazz musicians were also known to produce concept albums. Nat King Cole and even Frank Sinatra were a few of those artists.

This brings us to the iTunes Age where you can buy a single for a song (pun intended). If you like, you can buy the whole album, but the trend appears to be singles, most of which are downloaded to an iPod or other device to create playlists. Personally, I'm not a fan of playlists. I do confess to wearing my iPod headphones when I go to sleep and putting it on "shuffle." OK . . . so I'm not all that consistent. But I like the idea of full albums and especially concept albums. I'm a big fan of Pink Floyd's *The Wall,* and I love the tune "Comfortably Numb." But I bought the album because it was important for me to understand the entire context. "Comfortably Numb" makes much more sense when listened to as a part of the whole.

ARTISTS DOING IT FOR THEMSELVES

That's the end of today's history lesson. Now it's on to artists doing it for themselves . . . sort of. There are many, many opportunities for today's indie artists to do things for themselves in terms of recording, producing, distributing, and promoting. But a couple of things really stand out: artist and fan collaboration, as well as collaborations with other artists. That may have happened to a degree in the past, but it was mostly through fan letters and, perhaps, the occasional phone call to the right person, if that person could be found and reached.

With social media outlets such as Facebook, Twitter, MySpace, and ReverbNation, all of which have been discussed previously, the tides have turned. Hip-hop group The Bayliens are something of pioneers of this idea. They allow fans to remix their music in a way they (the fans) want to hear it. It's yet another way to engage your audience. Trifonic is another one. This site allows for downloads of various songs that fans can edit and remix. What better way is there to totally engage a fan than to have them be a part of the song-making process? Try it out at http:// ccmixter.org/trifonic.

The first cousin, or perhaps the parent, to all this is artist-to-artist collaboration. For example, Kompoz.com is a major collaboration site. Artists can create either public or private projects. Private projects allow only people you designate to be a party to the project. Plus, private projects have copyright licensing options that public projects don't. Public projects are open to everyone and, while still rich with features, they offer a creative commons licensing.

Based in New York City, another popular service is IndabaMusic. com, which was launched in 2007. The site boasts an impressive lineup of board members and advisors and a talented cast and crew. The purpose of the site is to create "a place for musicians around the world to network and make music together through online collaboration." It has "grown to over 700,000 musicians—from hobbyists to Grammy Award winners."

The site's platform offers an array of tools and services to help musicians network and provide education, production support, promotion, and distribution. The site offers a variety of opportunities in terms of contests and also licensing help and support. Plus, Indaba provides its members with a community of groups, featured artists, and message boards. Indaba also offers online sessions, mastering (starting at just $70/ track), and Mantis. Mantis is an application that allows you to create your own mixes and remixes and easily collaborate with musicians around the world. Features include the following:

- Record 16-bit/44.1K audio straight to your IndabaMusic. com account
- Mix with nondestructive, real-time effects
- Tap into a library of more than 10,000 sounds

- Access your mixes from anywhere with an Internet connection
- And much more

There are several other sites on the Net. Poke around and you'll likely find a service that's just a right fit for you.

NONTRADITIONAL PHYSICAL RELEASES

For the most part, if not the entire part, nontraditional music releases means digital releases. But it can also mean burning your own CDs. Let's start with the latter.

Here's a relatively simple idea: Write some songs, find a studio or place to record, rehearse, rehearse some more, do some production and mixing work, get the sound down, and make a master. Then what? How do you get your masterpiece into the fans' hands?

One option is to make your own CDs. If you're just making a few demos, you can probably get by with a CD/DVD burner in your computer or a peripheral. Beyond that, there are loads of CD duplication services online or even in your local office supply store. For example, Diskmakers.com offers a wide variety of packages, such as the Working Band Bundle at $1,229. The bundled package includes the following (according to the site):

- 1,000 CDs in full-color, four-panel Digipaks
- 100 download cards
- 100 11" x 17" posters
- Custom commemorative plaque
- Worldwide CD and download sales via CD Baby and iTunes
- Gracenote CDDB and Allmusic.com registration
- Huge 3' x 5' full-color vinyl event banner

A package like this can certainly jumpstart your efforts at a fairly reasonable price. The service also provides several printed marketing materials to help get the word out. Other services include MasterCopy (www.cdmastercopy.com), DiskFaktory (www.diskfaktory.com), and BeyondConcepts (www.bcduplication.com).

Other options are Web Keys and USB drives. In mp3 format, you can pop quite a bit of music on these at an affordable rate. They can be sold as merchandise or used as promotional giveaways. Many suppliers will brand your USB device with your logo and site address. This may be included or sold as an add-on service. A branded USB drive with your logo and site address can be a great tool to drive traffic, especially when these devices are shared with your fans' friends.

FANS: COLLECTORS VERSUS THE CAPTURE CULTURE

Collectors are, or were, just that. They bought 45s, vinyl albums, box sets, CDs, and the like. They built physical libraries of music. Great as it was, these days it seems a wee bit archaic. Sorting through miles of albums took a lot of time to find that "just right" tune for a romantic evening. Even more confounding was where to put all that stuff. If you were into music, finding a home for all those 45s, vinyl albums, box sets, and CDs took a lot of space. If you were blessed with a dedicated music room, maybe it wasn't so bad. Most of us weren't so blessed. Plus, unless you happen to be musically obsessive-compulsive, that library was more of a mishmash than something that would do the Dewey Decimal System proud. Oh sure, we'd try, but our organizational efforts would usually quickly erode into chaos. Nonetheless, back in those days, we had no other choice.

Another problem with the collector culture was finding the name of a tune. If a DJ didn't mention it, we were somewhat stuck until we heard the song again and, hopefully, this time the DJ would announce the title and artist. Humming a few bars to a friend usually didn't help too much, either.

By comparison, the capture culture focuses on digital delivery of music. An array of apps allows us to download what we want directly to our player of choice and pay for it electronically. To find a particular song or artist, you simply type in a search box. Voila! Many programs even provide the ability to bring in cover artwork, liner notes, and lyrics. How handy is that? And apps such as Pandora will even make suggestions for similar types of music you might enjoy. In addition, ID apps such as SoundHound instantly provide the name of a song, and you can also glean a wealth of information about the music, including the artist's bio, video sources, where to buy the music, lyrics, tour dates, and more. And now we don't even need to worry about hard storage on various devices. It's all going into the cloud and following us everywhere we go. Isn't the digital age wonderful?

All this neat stuff turns music from passive listening into an interactive experience. Owning music, in many ways, has become accessing music. Spotify, Facebook, and Pandora, along with many other platforms, are rapidly changing the way to access, listen to, and share music. And, to the labels' and retailers' dismay, the middleman is quickly becoming an entity of the past.

CLOUD-BASED SERVICES

Ah . . . the mighty cloud. Until recently, when you downloaded a song, it was stuck inside your iPod, iPad, smartphone, or other device. It was sort of handy, but moving tunes from here to there was, at best, a pain in the hindquarters. Not so anymore. The cloud is changing all that.

Industry analyst Aapo Markkanen is noted as saying, "The number of subscribers to mobile music streaming services is expected to approach 5.9 million by the end of this year [2011]." ABI Research believes that number will exceed 161 million subscribers in 2016, meaning a compound annual growth rate of nearly 95 percent. Sometime in 2012, the Asia-Pacific area will become the largest regional market for mobile music streaming.[10] That, dear reader, is nothing to sneeze at.

ABI, which focuses on the mobile perspective, also said, "Cloud computing is revolutionizing the digital music industry by shifting the consumer focus from ownership of songs to purchasing access to them in the form of on-demand streaming services. At the same time, the cloud is also being used to store owned tracks and albums and develop services that help listeners to discover a whole new range of music. Mobile handsets are a key driver of this change, due to their inherent portability and uniquely high penetration rate among consumers."[11] Moreover, cloud-focused folks tend to buy more music, and that's a good thing for the indie artist, whether solo or with a band. And retail prices are expected to come down. They will likely show a gradual decline as these services reach mass markets. Former practice director at ABI Neil Strother noted, "Forecasts of declining prices are based on the assumption that the rights-holders will lower their royalty demands. Record labels and collecting societies should not overplay their hands when it comes to royalty issues. If consumers do not have convenient and affordable legal alternatives, they will simply enjoy their music by other means."[12]

GETTING YOUR MUSIC INTO SPOTIFY, PANDORA, AND OTHER SERVICES

Spotify, Pandora, and other music services are big and will continue to grow as the capture culture increases. Getting your music into these services is not too tough, but like most things, there are a few hoops to jump through, and hopefully you won't get snagged in the process.

Spotify

Spotify is your new music collection. But unlike your old collector culture library, this one consists of millions of songs. And wherever you go, your music goes, too. Whether it's your iPod, iPad, smartphone, Mac, or PC, Spotify is there with you. Spotify also integrates with Facebook. If you've ever seen a post that tells you your friend is listening to this or that, it's probably from Spotify or one of its competitors. Click the link and you can listen, too.

That's the user's info. You're probably more concerned with getting your music into Spotify so the world can hear your tunes. First, you don't need to be a signed artist or have a record deal. The company recommends that you hook up with one of several third-party companies such as Record Union, CDBaby, Ditto Music, or Zimbalam to make your deliveries. They're also called artist aggregators. They will help you license your music and make submissions to Spotify as well as other outlets such as iTunes, Amazon, and 7digital. But, you'll need to create a standard agreement with these folks to make it all happen. For more information about aggregator and other music deals, visit semaphore-music.wordpress.com/tag/artist-aggregators.

DittoMusic.com is another one to look into. Here's some information about them from their site:

> From an idea born in a tiny Birmingham flat, Matt and Lee Parsons have helped over 30,000 artists distribute their music to a world-wide audience.
>
> In 2006, Matt and Lee wanted to release their own music independently. By the time they set up a record label, worked out barcodes and ISRC codes, and finally managed to get their music distributed, six months had passed. Their momentum stalled, their fans moved on, and their track limped into the charts at number 70. Their music career was over.
>
> With this setback came the realization that thousands of other artists must be feeling the same sense of frustration. So, with their newfound industry insights, Matt and Lee started releasing their friends' music. Artists paid a small upfront fee to cover operating costs, but they got to keep all the rights to their music, and 100 percent of the money from their sales. It was a small operation, but it would eventually change the way the music industry did business.
>
> In 2007 Matt and Lee were vindicated, releasing the first-ever UK top-40 single by an unsigned artist when Koopa's *Blag, Steal, and Borrow* entered the charts at number 32. Suddenly, Ditto was the hottest new music distributor in the world.
>
> Since then, Ditto has released eleven UK top-40 singles—all from unsigned artists—and artists like Price, Paul McCartney,

Finch, Suzi Quatro, Ed Sheeran, Maverick Sabre, Tupac, and Manfred Mann have all partnered with Ditto to get their music into as many digital stores as possible.

Ditto fees are fairly straightforward. A subscription for a single is roughly $8, and an album is $25, both paid annually. They also offer a variety of packages, from their Start a Record Label program priced at $41.25, to their Chart Breaker package priced at $130.35. More information can be found on their site at www.dittomusic.com/dittomusic/Custom.aspx?Services.

So, how much can you make? A fair question. Although it varies between countries and platforms, Spotify roughly pays $0.003 per play. By contrast, iTunes pays roughly $0.70/track. This is before any applicable taxes and added fees, so the amount you actually receive will be slightly less. Most pay by bank transfer or PayPal.

An even better explanation comes from Dan Reitz, musician, producer, educator, and trombonist for the band Ramforinkus. On Dan's blog (http://danreitz.com/blog-spotify-piracy/), he provides some insights into his experience with using Spotify, iTunes, and other outlets for his song "Friend in the Head."

If you are a frequent user of Spotify, you've probably heard the ad that says, "Piracy is so last year. Every time you listen to music on Spotify, you make money for the rights holders and artists." If you haven't, you will; it comes on about once every two hours.

Spotify is an amazing service, offering unlimited, free access to an ocean of recorded music. It's the closest thing to a perfect music app since the original Napster (the pirated version), but whereas finding a tune on Napster was totally dependent on who was online at a given time, Spotify's entire library is 100 percent there 100 percent of the time—and it's legal. It is an absolute game changer, a revolutionary product, and the fact that it has the support of the recording industry means it will be around for a long time. But it's a young product and a young company, and Spotify's claims regarding the revenue being generated for artists deserve thorough scrutiny. Does listening to music on Spotify really support the artists you listen to? Is it really better for rights holders than piracy?

The short answer: not really, at least not yet.

Because my band doesn't have a record label or any other stakeholder taking a cut of the revenue, we receive the entire payout from each service:

- iTunes (UK/EU) ~$1.22/sale
- iTunes (US) ~$0.76/sale
- eMusic $0.40/sale
- Rhapsody $0.01/stream
- Spotify $0.00378/stream

So, if you lived in the United States and purchased a copy of "Friend in the Head" on iTunes for $0.99, we would have received about 77 percent of the sale. This could add up pretty quickly; had we sold 9,900 copies of our song over that six-month period, we would have received a check for about $7,600 from iTunes. . . .

Spotify has a completely different business model than iTunes in that it is a streaming music service, not an online store. Each time someone streamed the song from Spotify instead of purchasing it outright, we received a little less than four-tenths of $0.01. That means someone would have to stream our song two hundred times in order for my band to have received the same $0.76 payout as a single purchase on iTunes. This does not add up in any meaningful way until you get into the hundreds of thousands of streams, although it is a marked improvement over the way artists were initially compensated by Spotify. (Lady Gaga received $167 after her song "Poker Face" hit 1 million streams on Spotify in 2009, or 1.67 thousandths of $0.01 per stream.) . . .

When confronted about their business model, Spotify vigorously refutes the idea that they are anything other than the next great revenue source for artists. In a recent interview, a Spotify spokesperson said, "Spotify is now generating serious revenues for rights holders; since our launch just three years ago, we have paid over $100 million to labels and publishers, who, in turn, pass this on to the artists, composers, and authors they represent. Indeed, a top Swedish music executive was recently quoted as saying that Spotify is currently the biggest single revenue source for the music industry in Scandinavia."

If that claim is true, it is certainly impressive, but there's a serious disconnect here between what they say and what artists end up receiving per play on Spotify. Most major labels keep a considerable cut of that $0.004 payout, and independent artists who release their own material generally don't have enough marketing power to attract the number of listeners it would take to make Spotify a better revenue generator than iTunes. In fact, I might argue that fans pirating our song "Friend in the Head" could do more for us had they used Spotify to listen to it. If 103 people had pirated "Friend in the Head" instead of streaming it through Spotify, those 103 people would possess a digital copy of the song, which means there are dozens of ways they could pass it along to others. They could burn it to CD and could email it to their friends; they could listen to it using any audio player, in any setting, and could easily transfer it between devices; they could convert it to any format, they could add it to a video, they could sample it, they could make it their ringtone, they could play it as house music at a theater or club, and they could broadcast it on their radio show. By listening to "Friend in the Head" in Spotify instead of pirating it, those 103 people could have shared the tune with other Spotify users and their Facebook friends, and could have added it to their Spotify playlists, but there's not much else they could have done that would help the song reach new people since music on Spotify can't leave the Spotify application, and you can't take the Spotify application with you without paying $10 a month for it. So as an artist in several independent bands, I don't see how Spotify is really better than piracy. Maybe it is for Elton John, but even then, are you really going to listen to "Candle in the Wind" 103 times? . . .

Don't think that I'm bitter. I'm not. Spotify represents the future of music consumption. I am not only happy that Spotify is an option for my own music; I also use it several hours a day, both for fun and for work. We are a culture of convenience, and nothing is more convenient than immediate, cost-free access to every song you've ever wanted to hear. And I've always been cool with music piracy, so I'm not too upset that artists aren't getting paid much from Spotify. My issue is Spotify's frequent claim that you, the music consumer, support artists by using their service. Spotify should not be advertising that their listeners generate revenue for artists when it takes nearly 300 streams of a song for one member of a band to be able to buy a cup of coffee at a bodega. This leads to an environment where a fan might choose to listen to a song through Spotify instead of purchasing it in a way that generates exponentially greater revenue for the musicians, like iTunes.

Until Spotify's business model is improved, it should be seen as just another free music service, like Napster and Grooveshark before it, and it should be known that the best way to support your favorite artists is to purchase their music at full-price— especially their self-released material—and go to their shows when they're in town.[13]

Also, Dan mentioned that those iTunes figures are for both ringtones and regular iTunes sales, and each has a different pricing system. In the sales reports, iTunes lumps both types of sales together, and he didn't know if he could separate them. The figure for iTunes across-the-board payments is something around 90 percent of the sale price to the rights holders. The $0.70 or so in my article is a little higher than what would be received through straight iTunes sales because ringtones have a higher price point.

Also, Ramforinkus is remastering their tunes for an upcoming album and will probably remove old versions from the Internet once it drops. To listen to what the band is up to, point your browser to www.ramforinkus.com.

Pandora

A child of the Music Genome Project, Pandora is listened to by more than 40 million users. That's a lot of people and a lot of opportunity for you . . . if you can get in. That will take some prep work. To give you an idea of the competition, Michael Zapruder, music curator for Pandora, receives roughly 400 to 800 songs every month. And the staff at Pandora listen to each and every one. That's a full-time job in itself.

Here are their recommended steps from their site:

- First, you need to have a CD copy of your music with a bar code. When a recording studio agrees to record and replicate an album, a bar code is often included in the fees. But watch out: It can cost as much as $99 to buy a bar code. Pandora recommends Nation Wide Barcode, which charges only $10 per code. You can get it the same day.
- Once your music has been reproduced into a CD format, Pandora requires that the music be available in the physical Amazon CD store. You will need to create an account for Amazon Advantage, but there are no fees to join. It costs $29.95 per year plus a 55 percent standard commission on the sale of your CDs. Don't forget to enter in all the information that Amazon lists about your music. Most important, you need to upload the cover art for the album.

- Speaking of albums, no matter how awesome all the other songs on a CD might sound, you need the rights to use every song on the album. Once Pandora accepts your music, they may use all the songs on your CD.
- It is also suggested that before submitting, you collect relevant information about your fan base, selling power, and music reviews. This will not help with the Music Genome Project, but it can be a good indicator to Pandora if people want to hear your music.
- Go to Pandora's submission form at submitmusic.pandora. com and give them all the information you have prepared. You will want to submit your best two songs from the CD you put on Amazon. Zapruder also suggests not putting in more than one submission until you know whether your first CD has been approved or denied.

By utilizing the wealth of musicological information stored in the Music Genome Project, Pandora recognizes and responds to each individual's tastes. The result is a much more personalized radio experience—stations that play music you'll love—and nothing else.

Do you get paid by Pandora? In a word, sort of. OK, that's two words, but you get the idea. To get your royalties, you'll need to register with SoundExchange. Pandora is more like radio than, say, Spotify. Here's the lowdown from their site: "SoundExchange is the nonprofit performance rights organization that collects statutory royalties from satellite radio (such as SIRIUS XM), Internet radio, cable TV music channels, and similar platforms for streaming sound recordings. The Copyright Royalty Board, which is appointed by the U.S. Library of Congress, has entrusted SoundExchange as the sole entity in the United States to collect and distribute these digital performance royalties on behalf of featured recording artists, master rights owners (like record labels), and independent artists who record and own their masters." So, a SoundExchange account is a needed thing if you want that mansion and Porsche.

There are plenty of opportunities to get out there and get heard, but it will take some work. That should be a big part of your business and marketing plans mentioned in chapter 3.

Music distribution is changing rapidly. Planning and getting your music, promotional efforts, and such in order now will help you greatly in being successful.

7

Media Relations

You're not going to get too far if nobody knows about you. This is where media relations comes in—aggressive media relations. The ability to have reporters, writers, authors, and editors tout your virtues is paramount. Getting your name in print is important to establish your brand, image, and, ultimately, recognition. A wee bit of controversy doesn't hurt either, as long as it's not way over the top.

The first thing to remember about media relations is that they—writer, reporters, editors, bloggers, and so on—don't give a hoot about you, unless there's a story in it for them. Everybody wants something. So give it to them. A release about your nifty new song will likely get tossed in the circular file. These folks are inundated with press releases, media kits, and various other requests. You need to find a spin. That might mean aligning your band or act with a charity, a pro-bono event, something politically outspoken—stuff like that. You need news that will turn a head or two. Three is even better.

BUILDING A MEDIA LIST

This first key to media relations is to know whom you're talking to in terms of reporters, writers, editors, bloggers, and others. That's going to require building a media list.

A sibling to your prospects and industry contacts lists, your media list is destined to become one of the treasured items in your marketing toolbox. It's a list of all the media contacts who are going to skyrocket you to stardom.

You could dig deep into your pockets and subscribe to a list. They're available from companies such as Bacon's, Cision, MediaListsOnline, and Vocus. But this book centers around low and no-cost techniques, so we're not going to go there.

One simple way to jumpstart your list-building efforts is a visit to your local bookseller and the research section of your local library. Peruse the titles in the magazine and newspaper racks at the bookstore. Grab a few titles and a cup of java. Jot down the publication name, contact info for key editors and writers, and the type of news and content they print. At the library, get chummy with the research librarian, who can become one of your best list-building friends. The librarian can point you to a variety of sources such as the Standard Rate & Data (SRDS). The SRDS is a group of books (and online resource) media buyers use to find publications and media in which to place their clients' ads. But you can use it to identify publications in your niche and gather contact info, type of content, and more. The *Gale Directory of Publications and Broadcast Media* is also available at most larger libraries.

Those are a couple of the brick-and-mortar methods. Because you're a 21st-century kind of person, you're probably interested in using that box called a computer to find media sources online. A tablet works well, too—no problem.

After you've identified some publications in which you'd be pleased as punch to see your name in print, fire up the ol' browser, swing over to their sites, and nab a copy of their media kits. A media kit, in days gone by, was usually a splashy pocket folder or 3D thingie (box or similar deal) packed with information designed to convince an advertiser to buy space in the publication. Media kits carry detailed info about the publication's topic(s), ad space pricing, production specs, reader demographic data (a handy bit for you), and, usually, an editorial calendar along with key personnel contact info.

I could write a rather lengthy dissertation, listing numerous places where you can gather media contacts online. But, as luck would have it, Jeremy Porter did it for me with his excellent article, "14 Free Resources for Building a Media List," on Journalistics.com. How handy is that? Visit blog.journalistics.com/2009/free-resources-for-building-media-lists for a wealth of useful information.

Your list is, and should be, a continuing effort. Contacts and media come and go, so you'll need to keep an eye on things to ensure your list is up-to-date.

Once you have some contacts, what do you do with them? Odds are, you'll be contacting them with a press release and/or a press kit (more about those later), maybe a demo or two, and other stuff. Here are some tips when making a first contact:

- Ensure you have the contact's name, title, and what they write about correct.

    That's pretty much a no-brainer.
- Plan what you're going to say to ensure you stay on topic and don't ramble.
- Give them a heads-up, by phone and quickly, before you send anything.
- Ask how they prefer to be contacted.
- Respect their time.

    In days gone by I worked at a few large newspapers. Trust me, editorial departments are crazy places, especially at deadline time. Plus, like many businesses, media folk are having to do more with fewer people and even fewer resources.
- As a corollary to the above, always ask if it's a good time to speak.
- Keep to the facts.
- Demonstrate your musical expertise and style when you can, but keep it brief.
- Never interrupt.
- Ask what you can provide them to make their job a little easier.

In whatever you say, try your best to add value. Keep away from irrelevant information and "puff." Journalists are hardly stupid. They've heard it all and can tell if you're full of hot air.
- Always be able to back up what you say with facts, figures, and hard data. Reporters love facts and figures.

Over time, if you can, provide journalists with meaty information full of facts, figures, photos, and demos. You'll position yourself, your act, and your business as a quality resource. When that starts to happen, you may just find the phone and inbox ringing with requests for quotes and interviews.

DEVELOPING A PRESS KIT

A press kit, sometimes also called a media kit, is a collection of information about a person, product, company, event, or, in your case, your act, sent to the media as a promotional tool. It's all the information a journalist needs to write about the glories of you in one convenient place.

Your press kit can be created in a few ways: hire a PR firm or freelance writer/indie PR pro or do it yourself. Although I create press kits as one of the ways I make some dough, I'm going to shoot myself in the foot and recommend that you do it yourself. You know . . . because much of this book is all about low- and no-cost marketing and promotion.

Developing your very own press kit may seem a bit daunting at first, but it's really not all that tough. You just need to get organized, make a list of tasks, and dig in.

Let's take a peek at the ingredients of a typical press kit.

The Backgrounder

This part carries historical information about the band, act, or whom or whatever the kit is about. You'll highlight your musical offerings, style, what makes you different, and why you exist. Include some highlights like special gigs, pro-bono events, and so forth. Add in your value proposition (what you bring to the musical table the others don't or can't, why you're important to your audience, and why they should listen to you) and maybe a mission statement (why the band or act exists and what you're trying to accomplish), and you're good to go.

Oh . . . and a quick word about mission statements: Make them authentic and relevant . . . please. I've read so many that try to sound overly intelligent or are so abstract they make little sense. Be authentic. Be yourself. But sell your act. Let me add in a bit of advice from brilliant adman David Ogilvy, from *The Unpublished Ogilvy*: "Never use jargon words like reconceptualize, demassification, attitudinally. They are the hallmarks of a pretentious ass."[14]

The Fact Sheet

The fact sheet is pretty much what the title says: a listing of specific features and benefits, statistics, research highlights, and such. Reporters love facts, so make it easy for them. The fact sheet may contain gig venues, musical style(s), key performances with audience numbers if possible, and so on. It includes all that quantifiable data.

Biographies

In some instances, you can address key bio information in the backgrounder, for example, if the kit is about an individual. In other cases, it makes more sense to create a "bios" page with a couple of paragraphs about each key player in the band. Each bio should list the person's instrument, other bands that person has played with, awards, key responsibilities, relevant education and experience, and the like. But keep it brief. A couple of paragraphs should do the trick.

The Act and the Music

This is a page or pages that outline your tunes, albums, merchandise, and similar stuff. In a business press kit, this would be the Products and

Services page. The main thing to remember here is focusing on benefits, not features. Lots of people get hung up with their offering's swell bells and whistles, but that's not usually what's important to writers and editors. They want to know what's in it for them and their readers and why they should care.

Past Press Coverage

Got press? Include it. Journalists are usually more comfortable printing something about you when they know somebody else took the risk before them. Reprints from magazines are handy for this, and they look better than copies with shadowy spine folds or crooked placement. You can, for a fee, request magazine reprints from publications where you've been featured. If you can afford it, it's the way to go. Professional reprints look a lot better than copies.

Press Releases

Toss in your most recent press releases to fill things out and bring the recipient up to speed with current news.

Photos and Graphics

These can be key band member photos, performance photos, logos, and such. It's whatever you have or can get to add visuals to a story. The media likes to punctuate stories with images, so help them out.

Images can be hard copies or digital, but the latter is preferred because most, if not all, publications are produced electronically nowadays. Make sure your images have high enough resolution for print reproduction. The rule of thumb is two times the line screen of the publication. You can find the information in the publication's media kit ad production section. For most magazines that means at least 300 ppi (pixels per inch). Newspapers use a coarser screen, so they can be 120 to 200 ppi. When in doubt, go higher. Images can go down in resolution, but not up without a loss in quality. High-resolution .jpg files are OK; .tif files are better.

Logos should be in vector format, such as an .eps or Illustrator file. Vectors are resolution independent and can be scaled up or down without any loss in quality. It's a good idea to provide both CMYK and spot-color versions. If you use the services of a graphic designer, the designer should know all about this. If you're on your own, *CMYK* stands for "cyan, magenta, yellow, and black." Those are the colors used in printing to create the illusion of full color. Spot color is a specific color of ink that aligns with an accepted color-matching system, such as Pantone. For example, Pantone 200 is a red. Pantone Reflex Blue is a deep blue. Color-matching systems ensure that colors are reproduced consistently across a variety of printed materials. And that was our print production lesson for the day.

Collateral Advertising Materials

These might be postcards, posters, flyers, brochures, or print ads,. A printed newsletter would come under this heading, too.

Media Contact Information

The big boys and girls have public relations firms and/or a PR department. But, if you're an indie band or solo act, this isn't likely to be you. Give the recipient several ways to contact you—phone, email, and fax, of course, but perhaps also Skype and other instant-messaging services too. I'd shy away from carrier pigeons. They tend to be a bit messy.

Physical Form

After you've collected and written all your kit's content, it's time to think about what it will look like. You have a couple of options here: hard copies or digital.

If you opt for a hard copy, you can go all out and have the thing commercially printed. You could also go broke. These suckers get expensive. To do it relatively cheap, swing over to the office supply store and scope out some nice pocket folders. See if you can find something unique with some character to it. First impressions count for a lot. The interior pages can be copies (clean copies, please) or printed on-demand off your inkjet or laser printer. Design a compelling label for the cover. Crack 'N Peel label paper stock is good for this. Just be sure it's applied straight on the cover. Toss in your photos, brochures, and other materials, and voila! You've got yourself a press kit.

To be frank . . . oh, wait, Frank's my father. To be honest, I don't like this method for a few reasons. First, it's time consuming. Second, stuff tends to fall out of pocket folders. Third, you're asking the journalist to rekey your copious copy. I mentioned doing what you can to make things easier for the writer. So, it seems hard copies are somewhat counterproductive.

Digital Form

Perhaps it's because I'm a certifiable geek who sits in front of a computer for sixteen or so hours each day, but I like digital. It's just plain ol' easier and usually less costly.

Create a folder and call it "My Band Press Kit" (where "My Band" is your band's name, of course), mostly because that's what it's for, and put it on your desktop. Depending on how much content you have, you may want to create subfolders for your images, graphics, and .pdf files of flyers and other printed material such as posters and ads, along with various content sections.

Take all the content that you created digitally in the first place and save it to the proper spot within your press kit folder. Although Microsoft Word's .doc or .docx is the standard program to use, you might consider something more generic such as .rtf format, just in case. Files in .pdf format are handy too and pretty much a standard these days.

You don't want to lose a press opportunity because a writer is on some whiz-bang proprietary publishing software and couldn't open your files or copy and paste your brilliant content.

You're going to burn the folder contents to a disk, so you want to give some quality thought to a disk label and a jewel case cover. If you have stellar graphic design skills that others will agree with, do it yourself. If not, you really should hire a designer. Sure, it's going to cost you some clams, but hey, we're talking image here. This isn't a place to skimp. You want to put your best foot forward. Plus, you or, rather, they can likely repurpose some existing graphics from other materials created for your act. That can save you some money.

Don't just copy the "Press Kit" folder to the disk and burn it. That's an extra step for the recipient. Remember what I wrote about making things easy? If you dump the folder on the drive, Joe Journalist has to open the disk, then open the "Press Kit" folder just to start to get to your content. Just select the files and folders and drag them to the disk to burn. This way your files and content folders will be at the root of the drive.

Some nice things about digital press kits:

- They're cheap to produce on CD or DVD. If you want to get really fancy, put them on a USB drive that has your logo and some other info like a tagline, contact info, and so forth. Adding a demo tune is a nice touch as well. Pretty snazzy, eh?
- The journalist can copy, paste, or export the content.
- They're usually less expensive to mail or ship in CD or DVD format.
- You can put the content on your site, and other outlets such as Facebook, for downloading.

  Downloading a digital press kit is free, and free is good. Well, free is good for you. It's bad when your CDs, merchandise, and such are free. We're trying to make some money here.

And there you have it. Press kits on the cheap with a minimum of headaches.

NURTURING MEDIA CONTACTS AND BUILDING RELATIONSHIPS

Just because you sent out a kick-butt media kit, it won't mean jack unless you follow up. These are the folks who can make you famous, or at least better known. Get chummy with them.

Always make a follow-up call or at least send an email to ensure your kit or release was received, but always respect the writer's time. When calling, simply ask if it's a good time to talk briefly. Ask if there are any questions you can answer or if anything wasn't clear.

When you have a story idea, pitch it first; don't just send it off. A pitch letter is a brief letter or email that explains the story concept and why it's important to readers. If you really want to get the writer's attention, invite him or her to lunch (on you) to discuss the publication's needs more than your needs. Be a resource. When possible, arrange for press passes to shows.

Odds are, your first few releases won't make it into the publication. It takes time for the writer to realize that you're a good, solid source of news. When that happens, you'll start to see your name in print. Give it some time. Be consistent, but not a pain in the hindquarters. Remember, you need writers a lot more than they need you.

CRAFTING QUALITY PRESS RELEASES

Most press releases are vain ramblings about the wonders of a company, band, or other entity. They're also boring. As I've mentioned a few times, people want to know what's in it for them. Sad but true nonetheless. So, your press releases need to be engaging and tell your story.

Press releases are the foundation of your publicity efforts. When writing releases, be sure they conform to accepted standard formats. To follow is the dissection of a release from Eric Knight.

News Release
Contact:
John Sanders
28 Records
rec28@aol.com
Phone: 305.934.3349

September 28, 2008
For Immediate Release

Eric Knight Debuts Across the Pond on First UK Tour

Los Angeles, CA: Los Angeles–based rocker Eric Knight embarks on his official first tour (dates below) of the UK starting in October. This will mark the first time Eric tours the region. Knight has been busy in rehearsals preparing for the shows as well as in pre-production to enter the studio to record his third album, titled *Delusions Of Grandeur,* due out in early 2009. Once Eric returns from the UK, he will begin work on the new album, and in between recording, he will be doing some mini-tours in Canada and on the West Coast with friends Chasing Saints, who share the same management. Once the CD is released, Eric will be on an endless national tour of the United States to support the CD and then back to Europe.

Eric Knight has also been lending his voice to several recordings for film and TV as of late. Two tracks will be featured on an upcoming, unnamed ABC pilot due out later this fall. In addition to singing Eric has been not only in the studio writing for his upcoming album but also writing and composing music for film and TV. "I'm a big fan of soundtracks and movie scores, and it was always in the plan and a personal dream of mine to score a film," says the singer. "I'm looking to get into independent film first and work my way up to a major motion picture—that would be a dream come true."

To find out more information, visit his website at ericknight-online.com.

For press inquiries, additional show dates, or more information on Eric Knight, contact John Sanders at rec28@aol.com or visit Eric Knight at

ericknightonline.com

myspace.com/ericknight

Eric Knight's UK Tour Dates:

Oct. 18, 2008 - Cavern Club / Liverpool, England

Oct. 19, 2008 - Queen Boadicea / Clerkenwell, London

Oct. 21, 2008 - Monkey Chews / Chalk Farm, London

Oct. 22, 2008 - The Castle / Notting Hill, London

Oct. 23, 2008 - Edwards Bar / Hammersmith, London

###

Let's take this apart and look at each element.

Contact:
John Sanders
28 Records
rec28@aol.com
Phone: 305.934.3349

This is the contact info and should appear at the top of the release—pretty straightforward stuff.

September 28, 2008
For Immediate Release

This section shows the date of the release and whether or not it can be published immediately. If it cannot be released right away, include the desired publishing date, such as "For release on or after. . . ."

Eric Knight Debuts Across the Pond on First UK Tour

Here's your headline. It should immediately tell the editor what the release is all about.

Los Angeles, CA

This is called the "dateline," and it's inserted at the beginning of the first paragraph. Ironically, the "dateline" isn't a date at all. It's the location of your office or where the news originated.

> *Los Angeles–based rocker Eric Knight embarks on his official first tour (dates below) of the UK starting in October. This will mark the first time Eric tours the region. Knight has been busy in rehearsals preparing for the shows as well as in pre-production to enter the studio to record his third album, titled* Delusions of Grandeur, *due out in early 2009.*

Lead off with the most important information. Think of the body of your release as an inverted pyramid, with less important information lower in the release. Editors tend to cut from the bottom.

Wind up your release with some background information about key people or companies mentioned in the release.

When you're drafting your release, put on your reporter hat. Reporters want to know who, what, where, when, and why.

[more] and/or

If your release is two or more pages, let the editor know by including [more] at the end of each page. Close your release with either "-30-" or "###," the customary symbols to say, "That's all, folks." Center these symbols at the bottom of the last page.

It's a good idea to contact the editors of the publications where you plan to send your news to find out their preferences for receiving releases. Some prefer email, others like plain ol' snail mail, while others like faxed releases. Contacting them also helps to begin a relationship.

As I mentioned before, don't freak out if your first few releases never make it into print. That's not too unusual. Over time, as editors come to see you as a consistent source of quality news, they'll start publishing your stuff.

BUILDING BUZZ

If you're consistent, people will begin to take notice and spread the word. Word of mouth is one of the most powerful tools, if not the most powerful tool, in a musician's PR toolbox.

Twitter and Facebook are great ways to build buzz, if you offer great content. Followers and fans become evangelists of sorts for your act and will tell others about you. Also, connect with influencers—people with a "name"—and begin to build relationships with them via social media. It might be tough at first, but give it time and don't be annoying or, worse, seen as a stalker. Offer quality thoughts, comments, links, and such. Be engaging. These are the people who can help you get the word out faster than any other way could.

MEDIA RELATION TOOLS FOR MUSICIANS

Help a Reporter Out (HARO, www.helpareporter.com) from PR pro Peter Shankman is one of the best tools I know of to develop media relations and get your name in print. Plus, it's free.

After you sign up as a source, you'll receive three daily emails, Monday through Friday, with requests from writers, reporters, authors, TV producers, and more looking for sources for their articles, stories, books, casting calls, and so on. I've been written up in magazine articles and books plenty of times because of following HARO.

One-Sheets and Onesheet.com

A *one-sheet* is just what it sounds like: It's a single sheet that carries your publicity information. It provides information about a musician, band, or artist. Often, a one-sheet is sent with a newly released or soon-to-be released CD to provide related information. A one-sheet is also referred to as a press sheet or a promo sheet.

Onesheet.com is something of a one-stop source for building sites and mobile apps. The service allows you to use your own domain name and is relatively maintenance-free. Content you post on various other sites is automatically brought in to Onesheet. Sites are also fully branded, and you can even add a store to sell merchandise. Naturally, there are "Like" and "Follow" buttons to connect visitors to your Onesheet site. Visitors who post comments on Onesheet are also automatically brought into Facebook. Various content can be set as "Featured" with the use of a handy widget. Plus, this array of features is free.

Onesheet also offers a "Pro" version where you can have a mobile app developed for your act, a customized navigation bar, browser and mobile icons, Google Analytics, and a dandy contact form.

There's a fourteen-day free trial for both versions, and the "Pro" version is just $4.99/month—not a bad deal for even the most cash-strapped act.

BandTown

BandTown.com is designed to keep fans up-to-date with where their favorite artists are performing. With its seamless Facebook integration, it makes doing that a snap. From their site:

> Fully integrated into Facebook, Bandsintown automatically creates 100-percent-real Facebook events for all upcoming dates and displays them on a Tour Dates tab on your fan page. Fans can RSVP, comment, and share with friends right from the tab. Artists can share events with other artists on the same tour and even display tour histories.
>
> Getting the word out has never been easier. Maximize exposure and increase engagement using Bandsintown's built in tools to promote your gigs through timeline, ticker, newsfeed, and

Twitter. Our Auto Promote feature is geotargeted and automatically promotes events throughout your entire tour, from presale to on sale.

Our completely customizable and easy-to-embed JavaScript and Wordpress plug-ins make it simple to sync tour dates, ticket links, and Facebook events to your official website or blog. Works on Ning, Tumblr and other platforms.

The site also offers the creation of "Specials," which are packages for special offers, VIP treatments, and exclusive deals. This helps to generate revenue beyond ticket sales. And packages can, of course, be purchased directly on Facebook.

If you're feeling adventurous, a search for "media tools for musicians" will yield many other tools that can benefit your media relations and social media activities.

Sonicbids

Sonicbids.com is much like the other services mentioned, but with a slight spin. Sonicbids can connect you to promoters, of course, but also to the people responsible for getting music into movies, airlines, shopping malls, TV shows, and more.

I know what you're thinking. "Ew! Elevator music." That's not what Sonicbids is all about, but it might sound that way at first. There's money to be made there—potentially lots of it. Tie that to the fact that many fans learn about new music via these alternate outlets, and it can mean a boon for your act. Fees are affordable, too. Their "Sonic" membership is just $4.99 per month, paid annually. Their "Supersonic" membership is $9.99, also paid annually.

Founder Panos puts it this way:

I came to America in 1991 from my home country of Cyprus to attend Berklee College of Music. I didn't think I could cut it as a guitarist, so I ended up studying Music Business, which led to an internship at a Boston talent agency. Within a year or so, in 1995, I found myself booking all the European tours for some of my idols, people like Pat Metheny and Chick Corea and Sonny Rollins—a jazzhead's dream.

I got the inspiration to start Sonicbids as a direct result of my experiences as an agent. Every week I was getting buried with press kits from many, many talented artists who wanted to get booked by us, but we just could not afford to take on. So I thought—and this was 1999 or so—"if you can trade stocks and buy books online, why can't you get a gig or book a band using the web?"

I quit my job, maxed out my credit cards, and launched Sonicbids on February 25, 2001.

The company's mission statement is as follows: "Our mission is to help create and empower an Artistic Middle Class through the use of innovative technology. We want Sonicbids to be a place where any band from any genre anywhere in the world can come to find and connect with any type of music promoter, licensor, or consumer brand—easily, effectively, and quickly."

Sounds pretty good to me.

The takeaway is that to be visible and ultimately successful, you must develop solid media relationships. These should be authentic and helpful to writers, reporters, and similar media people. Develop your list. Put together a killer press kit, make contact, write engaging press releases, and use the tools available to you. Find those outlets and services that are a right fit for your band or solo act. Does it take time? You bet. But so does writing songs, rehearsing, prepping for performances, and the like.

8

Promoting to Radio

You're in your car, driving down some lonesome highway at 2:00 AM. Maybe, like Tom Petty, you're singing *Runaway*, along with Del Shannon. Suddenly, your tune comes on the radio. You pretty much go nuts. Hold on, Sparky. Don't hit the brakes or, worse, the gas. Sure, your song's being played, but it's just a start. Getting on the radio isn't an easy task, but there are steps you can take to put your best foot, or song, forward.

You might be hearing that radio is a diminishing influence on music buyers. But that's a myth. At least it's still a myth at this point in time. Radio is still in the forefront of record sales and will likely be so for a while. It's a main gun in a label's arsenal.

Radio and the labels have a symbiotic relationship. They need each other. Labels need an outlet for audiences to hear their artists and, subsequently, buy records. Radio stations need a constant flow of new music to appease and entertain their audiences so that they can sell ads. So, it follows that if the label can supply great music that listeners love, the radio station builds its audience and can sell more ads, often for more money. There sometimes are a few shady deals, but in most cases the two work together toward a mutually beneficial end. Labels and radio stations, for example, might work together to host or promote a concert. Other times the label will fly an artist or band in for an interview or an in-store signing event. When it works, everybody wins and gets a piece of the artist's income. The artist wins, too, because of the promotional value. That can easily turn into ticket and merchandise sales.

In chapters 5 and 6, I discussed podcasts, Spotify, and Pandora. They're arguably the easiest ways to get on the radio, albeit Internet radio, and there are still those dang hoops to jump through. And there are plenty of listeners. But there are a few easier inroads. Here are a few.

College Radio

Beginning in the 1980s, college radio started to become a significant force for discovering independent recording artists and also introducing those artists to the general public. Many have gone on to become household names with huge fan bases.

In addition, college radio has a reputation for presenting practically all forms of music. Most of this music would never make it to the commercial or even noncommercial arena.

Kenny Love, in his article *College Radio: The Most Important Radio Level for Musicians*, brought up some interesting points about the benefits of college radio. It offers

- Far easier and faster access to airwaves
- Far more plentiful specialty and mix shows and programs
- Greater chances for both in-studio and telephone interviews to promote music releases
- More possibilities for station ID checks for further publicity
- Corresponding college campus newspapers that will more readily accept and support music aired on their campus stations for creating a campus-wide buzz
- A ready and built-in market in the campus community for repeated live performances to further support and supplement campus airplay and campus press coverage
- An opportunity for grassroots distribution through supplying both campus bookstores and campus music stores with music releases

Love included some other very interesting facts.

- There were 631 public four-year colleges and universities that had a combined student population of 6,236,455.
- There were also 1,835 private four-year colleges and universities with a combined student population of 3,440,953.
- Additionally, there existed 1,081 public two-year colleges with a combined student population of 5,996,701.
- Even further, 621 private two-year colleges hosted another 253,878 students.[15]

Love added, "This brings the average U.S. student population total to a whopping 15,927,987 minimum every year. And more people are attending some form of higher education than ever before."[16]

That's a pretty significant audience. A few of the better-known acts who tapped into college radio are R.E.M., 10,000 Maniacs, The Smiths, XTC, and The Replacements. So, the company's not too bad.

How do you get on college radio? Good question. Here's yet another list to help you out:

- Research and develop a targeted list of college radio shows and stations (phone numbers, email addresses, physical addresses, contacts, etc.).
- Develop a spreadsheet to use as a tracking system so that you can remember who you sent what, who the contacts are and when you talked with them, and so on.
- Call the stations to get the names of the musical directors and show hosts. Then call back at a later date and ask for them by name.
- When you talk, learn what materials they expect to receive (CDs, demos, press kits, etc.).
- Talk about your act, the kind of music you play, performances you've done, and so on (i.e., promote). But, as it's said, you have two ears and one mouth; listen more than you talk.

- Send off your stuff and then wait a bit. Make a follow-up call to verify receipt.
- Give it some time and then make another call to learn if they listened to your music and if it's been added to the rotation.
- Be polite, but persistent, to learn if your music has, in fact, been heard and added to the rotation.

Local Radio

Getting your music played on local radio stations involves pretty much the same procedure as it does for college radio. There are a few twists, though. It's best to send your materials via FedEx or at least Express Mail. It just looks more important. Morning shows are always looking for folks to interview. Have a local gig coming up? Give the musical director or show host a call and ask for an interview about the event. Try to get testimonials from fans or places where you've played. These can be call-ins. Finally, bring some doughnuts or other breakfast fare. It will be appreciated, and you'll generally be treated nicer. Finally, mention your site address and Facebook page. If you sell merchandise, mention that, too.

Commercial Radio

If you have your heart set on hearing your dark-as-night, angst-driven song, complete with tearful arpeggios and ear-shattering solos on the radio, nestled between Ozzy Osbourne and Alice Cooper—in a word, from my New York Italian vernacular, "fugetaboutit." As an indie act, it's simply not going to happen. Sorry. Sometimes the truth hurts.

Here's why. Commercial radio is, for the most part, a pay-to-play thing. It tends to be a shakedown—a racket, if you will. It's a very tightly secured industry. Deals are made on the basis of handshakes instead of quality contracts. Handshakes that often erode into broken dreams and broken promises.

As a matter of fact, here's yet another history lesson for you. The term *payola*, which is a combination of the words, "pay" and "Victrola," was coined for the music industry's practice of pretty much outright bribery to get songs played. From Wikipedia (http://en.wikipedia.org/wiki/Payola), "Under U.S. law, 47 U.S.C. § 317, a radio station can play a specific song in exchange for money, but this must be disclosed on the air as being sponsored airtime, and that play of the song should not be counted as a 'regular airplay.'" However, that's not always the case. Somewhere, a corporate headquarters, where the big wigs live, makes the track selections for commercial radio. Plus, those selections are often decided on based on who provides the best and most in terms of favors, vacations, junkets, money, nifty gifts such as drugs, and other seedy, seamy, and unsavory commodities and services. I think you get the idea. Feel like washing your hands?

Sure, you could hire a shady radio promoter for a ton of cash. Other options include a deep-pocketed label. As discussed, they're pretty tough to get, if not impossible. You could also tap out your savings, pull funds from your 401(k), max out your credit cards, and get a second mortgage to hire a heavyweight public relation person or firm. People do it all the time. Fame is a powerful elixir. But, all in all, your money is likely better spent on the lower-cost techniques and tools discussed within the pages of this book.

However, there is one more option. Some commercial radio stations have local shows that feature local performers. Just be sure your music style is a good match for the show. Send out a one-sheet, some photos, and maybe a video, and start playing dialing for dialogue.

An additional word and reminder about one-sheets is probably in order. A one-sheet is a sales sheet, usually developed for labels and distributors to help sell an album. It typically contains information about the band or solo act, various achievements, information about the recording of the album, track list, and other pertinent data that, hopefully, all fits on one sheet of paper. Ergo the name "one-sheet."

THE IMPORTANCE OF BAR CODES

If you plan to sell your music, whether an album, CD, or even a single, to distributors and retailers, a bar code is essential. As a matter of fact, most outlets won't even touch your tunes without one. Also, with a bar code, Nielsen SoundScan can tally sales.

There are plenty of places to buy a bar code. And, like many things in life, there are many places that will rip you off blind. They do this by selling you a bar code, but it's actually under their vendor code. In effect, they own it, not you. This is an outright violation of the Uniform Code Council Agreement. In other words, it's pretty darn illegal. It's never legit to sell, rent, loan, or transfer a vendor code to someone else. *You've got to get your own.*

A bar code can run you close to $100. CDBaby and a few of the other sites mentioned in chapter 6 can help you out. CDBaby guarantees that the bar code is yours, not simply purchased as a resold code. Pandora recommends NationWide Barcode (www.nationwidebarcode.com), which charges only $10 for a bar code. Here are some fun facts from their site:

- Nationwide Barcode has been verified and approved by George Laurer, inventor of the UPC Barcode. It is good for all products except books (which require ISBN) and pharmaceuticals.
- It provides unique EAN and UPC barcode numbers always—never reused or recycled ones.
- It offers lightning fast service: Place your order and get your EAN and UPC barcodes within minutes with fast, automated delivery.
- It has no annual fees, and no hidden charges—and the guaranteed lowest prices.
- It provides free phone or email support.
- It supplies UPC numbers, which are used in the United States and Canada and can be read worldwide, and EAN numbers, which are used in Europe, Australia, Asia, and South America.
- It includes an Excel spreadsheet with all of your barcode numbers.
- It uses EAN-13 and UPC-A graphics—EPS (scalable vector) and 600 dpi JPEG. Barcodes are provided at 1.5" x .8" (38.27 mm x 20.3 mm) and can be scaled +/-20 percent.

- It features Certificate of Authenticity/Transfer of Ownership. (*Be careful about this!*) You want to ensure that you own the barcode and not the vendor.
- It presents resources for sticker or label printing.
- It publishes a free e-book, *Barcodes Demystified—Info on Shipping Container Barcodes, Coupon Codes, Barcode Colors and Sizes,* which offers information on how to communicate with your retailers and other topics.
- Additional after-the-sale solutions include shipping container barcodes, QR codes, and free webinars.

To ensure the code is yours, it's best to buy it from the Uniform Code Council. Their contact information is 7887 Washington, Suite 300, Dayton, OH 45459 USA, Phone: 937-435-3870, Fax: 937-435-7317.

RADIO PROMOTION SERVICES

As mentioned, the radio industry can be somewhat suspect when it comes to making deals. Beyond this is the reality that audiences are rapidly moving to becoming part of the capture culture, downloading songs to various devices and listening to Spotify, Pandora, and the like. Rather than pay a publicist or PR person $1,000 to $1,500 every month with no guarantee of a return, you might consider trying out some alternate services.

iPluggers.com

iPluggers is a new online music publicist service that can be used by indie artists, providing they can get approved by iPlugger's A&R folks. The process is simple: Sign up for an iPlugger artist account. Select your genre(s)—up to three—and upload your release. Then request A&R approval. Once approved, select your release date. This is when you pay for your release. When your date is reached, your release will be sent to all stations that want your type of genre. After "plugging," you can get real-time insights as to which stations in which countries downloaded your release for airplay. Airplay is guaranteed, and iPlugger does offer refunds if it is unable to achieve airplay for you. iPlugger also features a variety of other services, including photos, discography, videos, and more. How easy is that?

How much does all this cost? A single will cost roughly $315. Up to eight tracks is roughly $450, and an album with up to fifteen tracks runs roughly $625. iPlugger uses Euros as its currency, so the conversions may be a bit off.

Jango.com is another great service and similar to iPlugger. It's Internet-based and boasts 7,000,000 listeners. You upload your songs and photos and choose popular artists whose music is similar to yours. Your music will be listened to by audiences who also listen to the similar artists you chose. Many may become new fans. You also receive reports addressing how your new fan base is doing. Jango reports to you where your music was played, as well as how it was rated by Jango listeners. You can learn what tracks are most popular, what countries listen the most, and more. Additional premium features include targeting by age, gender, and location. If you fare well, you might even earn yourself some bonus Jango Play Credits. They award up to 100,000 each week.

How much will all this set you and your band back? 250 play credits cost just $10. 1,000 cost $30, and 4,000 cost only $100. Not too bad. Plus, Jango has been written up in *USA Today, The Wall Street Journal, Wired,* and several other publications.

The take away is

- Be prepared. Have a crystal-clear idea of what you're trying to accomplish and why.
- Have all your materials prepared well in advance—100 to 200 CDs, one-sheets, photos, bios, discography, press kit, news releases, recent press coverage, and so on.
- Carefully target your best prospects and use a spreadsheet to keep track of activities.

- Ensure the stations match your genre of music. If you play metal, don't contact a country station just because it's a radio station.
- Target college radio first.
- Call first to get the names (including the correct spelling) of the musical director and show hosts.
- Call back a few days later, asking for them by name.
- Promote your act, explain your genre of music, and highlight events you've played, but listen more than you talk.
- Send your materials via FedEx or Express mail.
- Call to verify receipt.
- Wait a few days, then call again to ensure that your music has been listened to by the host or others.
- Be polite, but be persistent.
- Buy your own bar code, and ensure that it's in your name.
- Investigate various radio promotion services and learn which is your best bet.
- Set aside a budget for radio promotion activities and fees.

Public and media relations are usually less expensive options to promote your music. But an even bigger plus is that PR is more believable than advertising. For example, let's say you're thumbing through a glossy city magazine and come across an ad for a cosmetic dentist on a right-hand page. It's full-color and pretty splashy. It certainly grabs your attention. Then you look at the left-hand page. There's a heart-warming story about an altruistic dentist who fills cavities in the teeth of underprivileged kids on a couple Saturdays each month. Which piece is more believable? You know the dentist on the right shelled out a load of dough to buy that slick color ad. He or she likely hired a professional copywriter to craft some poignant prose and a graphic designer to put it all together so your eyes would stop in their tracks when you saw the ad. But the story about the dentist on the left-hand page almost brought a tear to your eye. Odds are, you'd tend to believe the story rather than the ad. Yet that story was probably written by a PR pro and ended up in the publication due to the PR pro's relationship with the editor of the publication. And it more than likely cost a lot less, overall.

Publications need to fill their pages. They typically work on a percentage of news to ads. For example, a city magazine might run 30 percent ads and 70 percent news stories. Many tap into the services of freelancer writers and public relations firms for content that would be of interest to their readers. This is particularly important now, because ad revenues have been continually declining over the years, and many pubs don't have the budgets they used to for staff writers, photographers, and so on.

Unless it's a "shopper" type of publication, the stories get in for free. Shoppers often sell packages that include a cover image and a story written by their staff. Those are generally tied to an ad and can be pricey when all is said and done. They're also to be avoided. We're going for low- and no-cost marketing, PR, and promotion.

By having clear goals, a captivating story to tell, and a solid relationship with some key editors, you can reap the rewards of public relations, get your act promoted, help build your fan base, and sell tickets and merchandise.

9

For the Pure Songwriter

Maybe you're not the performing type. Getting up on stage might scare the hell out of you. But you love music, and you love to write songs. If so, this chapter's for you. Aside from the mundane, trite, and boring music that often assaults our ears, songwriting is about what's in your heart and mind. Then it's about constructing lyrics and a melody that communicate and resonate with an audience. It takes study, experimentation, talent, and a bit of luck.

Usually, the biggest challenge with writing song lyrics is where to start. That's typically followed by the common feelings most writers experience: "Is my idea any good, or does it suck?" "What do I do next?" "What if nobody likes it?" Relax. Most, if not all, songwriters go through this exercise. For the most part, if you like your song, it's probably good—at least good enough for you. If a whole bunch of people like it, it's probably more than good, maybe even great. And it might just make you some money.

But let's start with some background. Take the Brill Building for example. It's located on Broadway in New York City, just uptown from the Tin Pan Alley area and near Times Square. For many years, Brill housed music industry offices and studios, and some of the most iconic songs were written within its walls. In many ways, it was a musician's haven; an artist could find a publisher and printer, cut a demo, promote the record, and cut a deal with radio promoters, all within the

Brill building. Aldon Music, founded by Don Kirshner and Al Nevins in 1958, was one of them. It wasn't originally in the Brill Building, but was down the street a bit. Yet, Aldon was always connected to Brill. In many ways, it was something of a music mill, pumping out hit tune after hit tune, with songwriters working in cubicles or from home. Artists including Neil Sedaka, Howard Greenfield, Carole King, Gerry Goffin, Neil Diamond, Paul Simon, Phil Spector, Barry Mann, Cynthia Weil, and Jack Keller were all associated with Aldon. That's a darn good lineup.

Neil Sedaka, a guy who wrote or co-wrote more than 500 songs and sold millions of records, wrote the iconic song *Oh! Carol* there. It was about his girlfriend at the time, Carol Klein. Carol went on to become Carole King, a prolific songwriter and performer in her own right, who won four Grammy Awards and was inducted into the Songwriters Hall of Fame and the Rock and Roll Hall of Fame. Aldon made for good company, even though many writers were staff writers and didn't make as much money as they should have. But that's just my opinion. Later in life most of these writers/performers made a ton of dough. So, I guess things work out in the long run.

Most of the people mentioned in the previous paragraphs wrote words and music. Then there are the lyricists. They write, but they don't perform, in most cases. These are the folks whose job it is to write the words that make you laugh, cry, bring back a memory or moment in time, and cause their words to play over and over and over again in the depths of your brain. (This would also be known as a "hook." But more on hooks in a few paragraphs.)

Ira Gershwin, Bernie Taupin, Howard Greenfield, Barry Mann, and Tim Rice come to mind immediately. Paul McCartney, John Lennon, and Bob Dylan, although also performers, are certainly also on the list of some of the greatest lyricists. As a matter of fact, pure lyricists are somewhat hard to find. There are plenty of singer/songwriters. But lyricists? Not so much.

Lyricists are poets of a sort—wordsmiths. They spin memorable words that tie seamlessly into a song's genre, theme, length, and rhythm—not exactly an easy task. For example, I'm a writer. (You probably figured that out already.) I've tried writing lyrics, but they, in a word, stink. I'm not a poet. I'm not a Byron, a Keats, or a Shelley—or a Taupin for that matter. I'm not even in the same city as the ballpark. I'm strictly prose, it seems. (Insert heavy sigh here.)

WHERE TO START

In the immortal words of Glinda, the Good Witch of the North, "It's always best to start at the beginning." For most lyricists, that means a melody. It's tough to write lyrics without knowing the rhythm and other characteristics of the tune.

Once you have a melody, even a rough one, listen and pick out the areas where the notes are repeated or "rhyme." A better way of saying that is the places where the notes or chords are repeated in sequence. For example, let's use "Unchained Melody" by The Righteous Brothers. Who, by the way, may have been righteous, but they sure weren't brothers. Their name actually came at the end of a U.S. Marine per-formance when a fan in the audience shouted, "That was righteous, brothers!" Isn't trivia neat?

Alas, I digress. Back to "Unchained Melody." The rhymes happen at various, predictable intervals within the tune. It's the device that forms the structure of the song. The beat follows the rhyme in many cases. For example, "touch" rhymes with "much." "Time" rhymes with "mine," and so on. It also happens to a degree in the final line of the chorus.

As I write the above, it occurs to me that all this sounds rather com-plex. Relax. It's not. It's an ear thing. Listen to the melody, and it will become quickly apparent where the rhyme needs to come into play. The trick, and there's always a trick, is to find the right words that not only rhyme but also make sense within the context of the song's concept. And not all songs even need to rhyme. "Breakfast at Tiffany's" doesn't rhyme. Neither does "Strawberry Fields Forever." For that matter, 10,000 Mani-ac's "These Are Days" doesn't have a chorus. Rules were meant to be broken, so it would seem.

WHAT'S NEXT?

A title is always a good idea. Several lyricists start with the title and go from there. For others, the title becomes apparent after the song is completed or at least partially completed. Often, the sheer emotional value of the melody will help determine a title. Give this some time. Inasmuch as it's said that a book shouldn't be judged by its cover, it often is, and it's reflected in the sales numbers. In a similar vein, the title of a song can help sales. Does it immediately connect with an audience? Can they relate to it? Can they put themselves into the title and, ultimately, the song? Bryan Adams' "Summer of '69" did that for me. That was the time of my youthful follies, the girl I was totally in love with, and all the crazy nonsense my band mates and I managed to instigate. The rest of the song simply confirmed all that for me. For me, "Summer of '69" said it all. And to think, it started out as the "B" side of a single. Other titles that captured me are Death Cab for Cutie's "I'll Follow You Into the Dark," Floyd's "Comfortably Numb," and, at the time, Alice Cooper's "I'm Eighteen." Now that you've had a brief tour into my warped psyche, let's move on.

With a melody in hand and a title, it's time to get to work. And, make no mistake, it is work. Your lyrics need to be compelling, tell a story, and work with the melody and composition of the song. Whereas a poet does much the same, the poet doesn't have the musical bits to contend with for the most part.

Start with a rock-solid idea of what the heck you're trying to say. Leonard Cohen is a great example of this attribute. He nails it. By listening to his music, it seems to me that Cohen has a vividly clear idea of what he wants to say . . . and then says it or, rather, writes it. His style centers on themes. Cohen's work involves love, sex, religion, depression, and music itself. He's a man with a message, and one who knows how to tell it in an engaging way.

The first time I heard "Hallelujah," it tore me up. From Wikipedia (en.wikipedia.org/wiki/Leonard_Cohen):

Cohen's lyrical poetry and his view that "many different hallelujahs exist" is reflected in wide-ranging covers with very different intents or tones of speech, allowing the song to be "melancholic, fragile, uplifting [or] joyous" depending on the performer: The Welsh singer-songwriter John Cale, the first person to record a cover version of the song in 1991, promoted a message of "soberness and sincerity" in contrast to Cohen's dispassionate tone; the cover by Jeff Buckley, an American singer-songwriter, is more sorrowful and was described by Buckley as "a hallelujah to the orgasm"; Crowe interpreted the song as a "very sexual" composition that discussed relationships; Wainwright offered a "purifying and almost liturgical" interpretation to the song; and Guy Garvey of the British band Elbow anthropomorphized the hallelujah as a "stately creature" and incorporated his religious interpretation of the song into his band's recordings.

To me, it's just a great song that summed up what I was feeling at the time I first heard it.

Like Cohen, singer and stellar songwriter Joni Mitchell is another one who hits home. Allmusic said, "When the dust settles, Joni Mitchell may stand as the most important and influential female recording artist of the late 20th century and *Rolling Stone* called her 'one of the greatest songwriters ever.' Mitchell's lyrics have been noted for their developed poetics, addressing social and environmental ideals alongside individual feelings of romantic longing, confusion, disillusion and joy."[17] Joni knows what she wants to say and says it with grace, style, and elegance.

With your title decided, some questions need to be answered to develop the lyrics. Because songs are essentially sonic stories, composing them is much like writing a book or at least a detailed article. So the typical reporter rules apply: who, what, when, where, and why.

With Cohen's "Hallelujah," the who, it seems, is actually several Biblical characters—David and Samson, along with Bathshebva, who David saw bathing on the roof and, apparently, Samson's Delilah, from the "cut your hair" reference. But there's another person to whom Cohen is talking. The person who doesn't care for music.

The "what" seems to be the imperfection of man. David screwed up. Samson screwed up. We all screw up. The "where and when" is, for the most part Biblical times, yet also modern times because Cohen is speaking to another person, presumably a lover. The "why" is "Hallelujah." It's the cornerstone of the song. Hallelujah means an exclamation of praise to God. So, it seems to me that the song is about man's failing and his praise to God for helping out here and there.

Another classic is Joni Mitchell's "The Circle Game," a great, albeit somewhat tearful, tune. The "who" is the child. It might be a boy or girl, but I prefer a boy because I used to sing my son to sleep while playing the song. The "what" is the child journey through childhood to adulthood. The "where" isn't really relevant. It's where the child grew up. It might be Joni's backyard for all I know. The "when" is the child's youth and its passing on to becoming an adult. The "why" is the reality that we really can't look back. We can only live with what we have now and, hopefully, make the best of it and create wonderful memories. Dreams and hopes change along the way. As she says, maybe they'll be "better dreams and plenty." "The Circle Game" tells the story of all of us, and Mitchell says it with pointed elegance.

SONG STRUCTURE

Typical song structure consists of a verse, a chorus and sometimes a pre-chorus, the bridge, and the mysterious "middle eight." Other elements can be solos and a bit called the "collision."

The verse and chorus are what many of us think of when it comes to a typical song. The verse is the main part of the song. It's the words and melody that tell the story. The verse changes throughout the song as it progresses. The chorus is the part of a song that repeats throughout the tune. The lyric is usually the same.

A bridge, often found nearer to the end of a tune, can be described as something of a transition. It's an optional bit, but can add interest to a song and help keep the listener engaged more than just verse, chorus, verse. The bridge generally appears only once during the song and can be a different chord progression, tempo, or even key. After that, the song returns to its roots in verse and chorus.

The middle eight is something that throws a lot of people, musicians included. The term is at times used interchangeably with bridge. But it is a different animal. The middle eight normally appears in the middle of a song and is typically eight bars long—hence the name. Beyond that, it's a departure from the rest of the song. It may be in a different key or chord pattern. Sometimes it adds energy. Other times, it slows the song down. All in all, like the bridge, it keeps the listener engaged and adds interest because it's often unexpected.

A good example of middle eight use is in Sting's "Fields of Gold." After four verses, the chords change and the verse, "I never made promises lightly . . ." enters the picture. It enhances the tune by revealing broken promises to the singer's lover. It's an abrupt surprise that adds to the story. Other times the middle eight is not lyrical. It can be an unforeseen musical change in tempo or key or a combination of elements.

A solo is just that. It's an instrumental solo by a single performer. The collision is when different parts of a tune overlap. It's generally short and designed to create a sense of tension.

That musical theory lesson brings us to the ever-popular "hook." It's the part of a song that get burned into your brain cells and, like a broken mp3 player, it plays over and over, usually in the shower or some utterly inappropriate place, like a business meeting or a date with a stunning woman or strappingly handsome guy. Such is the nature of a good hook. It hooks you completely. You're trying to concentrate and all you can think of is that dang song. Over and over and over. . . .

The hook is usually found in the chorus as a short riff or lyric. It's the part of a piece that stands out and practically screams, if not literally, as in Springsteen's "Baby, we were born to run." Other times the hook can be instrumental, as in Deep Purple's "Smoke On the Water." A simple riff, but utterly memorable.

Now comes the tough part—putting all this together, lyrically. Beyond verse, chorus, bridges, hooks, and the like, the lyrics need to flow, make sense, and, most important, be singable. Your idea might be great, but if it's choppy or contains difficult words or phrases, it's going to be a difficult task for the singer. Words should roll off the tongue. Avoid too many stops. The listener might lose interest. You certainly don't want listeners confusing your hard-worked lyric or, worse, the singer. Consider folks who mistook Madonna's "Like a Virgin." Many thought the lyric was "Like a virgin, touched for the thirty-fourth time." Or consider Queen fans' faux pas from "Bohemian Rhapsody": "I see a little silhouetto of a man, scare a moose, scare a moose, will you do my fan Van Gogh?" Others thought it was "Scallaboosh, scallaboosh, will you do the banned tango?" And who could forget the "Purple Haze" mess up, "'Scuse me while I kiss this guy"?

Sometimes it's a good idea to use words or phrases with the rhythmic sound you want, even if you don't have the right words yet. Paul McCartney did that with "Yesterday" (although credited as a Lennon/McCartney creation). The working title was "Scrambled Eggs." That makes sense because, rhythmically, it sounds like "yesterday." As a matter of fact, McCartney is noted as saying, "I did the tune easily and then the words took about two weeks."[18]

ACTUALLY WRITING LYRICS

Before jumping in and writing lyrics, unless you're innately talented, listen to a lot of the types of songs you'd like to write. Dissect them. How and why do they work? What does the title suggest, and how do the lyrics answer that suggestion? Remember, your listeners know nothing about the song, story, or concept the first time they hear it. Often they don't know until they've heard your song a few times. Sadly, others will never get it.

Write a little bit at a time and give yourself time to digest it. Usually, new and often better ideas will crop up. I do this with my writing and my design work. I do a bit and then walk away to do more important things like play Solitaire or check out what's happening on Facebook. For design stuff, I do a few layouts and stick them up on the wall. Then I give it a few days before I revisit things. If you lose your momentum, don't sweat it. The song's not going anywhere. Unless you're under a label contract or writing for commercial applications, there's usually not a deadline. Chill out. It's your song. It's your time. It will come. Most important, don't force things. Avoid, like the plague, words that don't work just because they happen to fit into the structure or rhyme nicely. Your song needs to make sense, after all.

CREATING AND SUBMITTING DEMOS

After a bit, you'll have a song—maybe two or three. If you're really on a roll, you might have written an entire album's worth. If you're happy with your songs and others are, too, it's likely time to make a demo. Here's where things start to get tricky and potentially expensive.

For the indie songwriter, all the other stuff in this book applies. You need a social media presence, a site, a press kit, a media list and contacts, and all the rest. The only difference is that your spin will be a little different. One of the biggest differences is making a demo. Bands and solo artists can make their own with their own equipment or by renting some studio time. Songwriters need someone to perform their master works. If you're also a player with a wee bit of confidence, you might be able to create your own demo. If you don't have the playing ability to match your stellar lyrics or don't have the right equipment, you're going to need to hire a pro or at least some musical friends. The latter is preferred, if they're good and can do justice to your song and have the right equipment. It will be less expensive in the not-too-long run and you can likely work out a barter deal. You both get demos for your promotional efforts.

A Word about Copyright

Once you have a demo and you're pleased as punch with the production, before you do anything else, have your work copyrighted to protect yourself. I know it's hard to believe, but there are some unsavory and unscrupulous people out there more than willing to steal your hard work. Copyrighting your lyrics and complete songs is fairly painless, but it will cost you a few bucks. On the up side, you can copyright several works under one submission. Here's how it works:

- Visit www.copyright.gov. Be sure to read the "About Copyright" section so that you can become familiar with how the process works.
- Pull out your credit or debit card. Registering a copyright will set you back roughly $35.
- Click the "Electronic Copyright Office" link with the odd "e" icon. That will take you to a page with information about electronic registration and the old-fashioned paper and snail mail method. I'd opt for the electronic method. This is the 21st century, after all.
- Read everything on that page. For that matter, read everything you can on the site to gain a thorough understanding of copyrights and what you're getting yourself into.
- Next, click the "Electronic Copyright Office" link at the end of the top "eCO Online System" section. That will take you to a page that addresses security and privacy. Read that and then click the "Continue to eCO" button.
- If you're a new user to the system, click the barely visible "If you are a new user, click here to register" link. There you'll set up your account, password, and such. Be aware: The copyright office has strict rules for passwords. You may need to try a few before you find one that works.
- After you get through all that (which sounds a lot worse than it is), you'll land on the main copyright registration page.
- In the left-side navigation, click "Register a New Claim," fill out the forms, and fork over some dough.
- The form you want to register for lyrics is Form PA (performing arts), which can also be downloaded at www.copyright.gov/forms/formpa.pdf.

- Also note that you can use the option of registering several works under one application. An example might be "The Collective Lyrical Works of the Best Lyricist in the World, 2012." At just $35, it will save you some moolah, and you'll still be protected.

I know this all sounds really complicated, but it's not. Well, except for that dang password deal. Have a few variations ready to copy and paste from a word processor and save the username and password. Did I mention to save your username and password? Trust me, doing so will get you out of a jam. I keep roughly 500 passwords and usernames for me and my clients. Most are in my head, but they're also in a spreadsheet. You'll get busy doing stuff and, at some point, you'll forget the information. It happens. So save the darn stuff.

SELLING YOUR LYRICS . . . OR NOT

When it comes to selling your lyrics, you don't really sell them. Well . . . you can sell them or, rather, the copyright, but traditionally, lyricists get paid for playtime. In other words, you get paid when songs are recorded, played on the radio, and sold as CDs. It's typically a whopping $0.092 for each copy sold, and that's a 50/50 split between you and your publisher. Naturally, because you're *just* the lyricist . . . *the creator of the work* . . . the royalty check goes to your publisher. I guess they think we creative types can't be trusted with money. Your publisher will, or at least is supposed to, send you a check, typically each quarter. In the biz, they call this mechanical income. More on mechanical rights and income a bit later.

Most of the royalties come from radio and TV play. To help ensure things stay legit and you do get paid, there are a few organizations that track song plays. BMI, SESAC, and ASCAP are the majors and really the only ones worth their salt. These folks have affiliates all over the planet that track when your song is played—all over the world, that is, except for Russia and China, which don't honor copyright. Gee, what a big surprise.

(A little side note: You may have noticed I have something of a sarcastic streak in me at this point.)

These organizations, called Copyright Collective Organizations or Performing Rights Organizations (PRO), send you or your publisher a check each quarter with royalties for your songs' airplay. How nice is that? Walk out to the mailbox one fine, sunny day and find a hefty check. It's only going to be hefty, though, if your song is killer and gets a ton of airplay. And, as always, there's a catch. Should you join one of these organizations? If so, when should you join? Plus they have requirements. There are always requirements. Theirs are (1) that there is money to collect for your musical works, and, more important, (2) that you meet their requirements to receive money after you join.

Moses Avalon makes some good points in his article "Why You Should Think Twice Before Joining ASCAP, BMI, or SESAC." Avalon says, "So, unless one of the PROs offers you a financial incentive to join, you should wait until you have written music that fills at least one of the following criteria:[19]

- It was recorded by a significant artist, and the album or single is to be released in the next few months.
- It was placed in a movie soundtrack that is about to be broadcast on a major TV network in the next few months.
- It was used as a theme for a series that is about to be broadcast on a significant TV network in the next few months.
- It is currently getting a lot of play on a commercial radio station or podcast, or it has been tracked by a reliable service as being downloaded (legally) many thousands of times.

The full article, a two-part series, can be found at mosesavalon.com/why-you-should-wait-to-join-ascap-bmi-sesac/. Be sure to read the comments as well.

Now it's time to take off your lyricist's hat and don your sales hat. Sorry—it had to happen at some point, and that point is now. Who can you persuade to hook up with to get your songs out into the world?

Sometimes it might be an outright sale. Other times your song or songs can be licensed. For my money, licensing is often a better deal. You maintain the copyright, and, depending on your contract, you can re-license or sell the same tunes to other entities, such as

- Music publishers

  Music publishers generate income from your songs by getting those songs recorded by various bands or solo artists. They'll also tap into the television and film market. These are the people who hoof it, pitching your tunes.

- Record companies

  I also have referred to these companies as "labels." They're in the business of directly or indirectly producing and selling music, typically albums. If the artists in their stable don't write their own material, their A&R crews will scope out songwriters, usually through music publishers, to find the next hit for their artists.

- Producers

  Record producers oversee the entire recording, production, mixing, and mastering process. In addition, they often choose the songs that will eventually be on an album. Many are musicians or composers in their own right and have the ability to bring new ideas to a record.

- Ad agencies

  Many radio and TV commercials, also known as "spots," use jingles. Somebody has to write those jingles. It might as well be you.

- Films, TV, shows, plays, and so forth

  Musical directors are usually the people who make the decision to license a song for a show, whether it be a film, TV show, or Broadway extravaganza. They typically work for a production studio or through a management/talent agency. Check the credits at the end of films and TV shows. Their names will be listed, but they tend to fly by pretty quickly. Once you have some names, google them to find contact information.

It should be noted that licensing agreements can be tricky things with loads of details and legalese. It's best to hire an attorney who is familiar with licensing to help ensure that you get a good and fair deal.

10

Merchandise Sales

If you've got some gigs, you've got an opportunity to increase, if not double, your performance fee, especially at a smaller venue. The word is "merchandise," also known in the business as "merch."

Bands and solo acts can make a ton of dough by selling merchandise. As a matter of fact, merchandise sales can often do much better than CD sales. Your fans love to buy stuff emblazoned with your stunning logo and other cool graphics. Actually, "fans" in this case might not be the best word. The word "customers" comes to mind. And that they are, so treat them as such. Offer them as great an experience at your merch table as they have at your show. Customer service counts for a lot. Have your table crew be courteous and respectful. Be ready to answer questions. Be nice.

There's all sorts of merch, but wearables, such as T-shirts, hats, and so on, outnumber the bulk of them. What could be better than having your fans . . . er . . . customers . . . pay you to advertise your act? That's the beauty of merchandise. Your fans get cool stuff to wear or show off. You get money and extra promotion. All is well with the universe.

You don't even need to be a big name act to pull off this miraculous task. All you need are some fans, a venue, and a table. If you can have one or more members of your street team man the table, that's great. What's better is if the band members or solo artist makes an appearance to help sell some stuff before or after the show. After is likely a better option.

The fans are pumped, and it's much easier for them to dig deep into their pockets and pull out some cash or plastic (more on plastic possibilities later). After a stellar performance (and it should always be stellar), fans are fired up. Passing by your (highly visible) merch table can have them craving a T-shirt, hat, or other item. You might even consider doing a CD or shirt signing—or, in some stranger cases, a body part signing. Yup, it happens. So bring a few Sharpies.

When somebody first asks for your autograph, it's a pretty weird experience, albeit a good one. The first time it happened to me, I was speaking at a conference and walking through the center with another speaker after our talks. A couple of delightful young ladies came up and asked for our autographs and asked if they could have a photo taken with us. I was stunned. My first thought was, "You poor, poor misguided souls." The thing is this: To you and your friends and family, you're just you. To your fans, particularly dedicated, loyal fans, you're something more. Yeah, it's weird, but that's the reality. Treat your fans like royalty. When you do, you have a pretty good chance of turning them from loyal fans into evangelists for your act. They'll tell friends, spread the word on social media, and get you a lot more promotion than you could ever do alone.

But there are potential pitfalls to selling merchandise. First, merch costs money. You might make it up at a couple of shows, but you'll need some upfront money to buy the stuff you're going to sell. This is a basic law of economics. You know, that class you utterly hated in school? Well, now it's coming back to haunt you. And here you thought all you needed to do was be creative. Yeah. Right. Music is a business, and you're in business to make money—hopefully, a lot of it. Creative freedom and satisfaction don't come too easy when you're worried about money, paying the rent, and where your next meal is coming from. It's all about supply and demand and the fact that it takes money to make money. So, put a merch budget aside from the revenue generated from a few gigs and CD sales, along with initial merch sales.

Next, your merch should not be junk. Junk does not sell. Repeat after me, "Junk does not sell. Junk does not sell." Make that your mantra.

Your merchandise must be on par with your performance, at bare minimum. Ideally, it should be even better. Beyond that, it's a good idea to have levels of merch, or items at various price points. The low end might be a branded keychain, then hats or similar middle-of-the-road items. Then comes USB drives with a song or two, followed by higher-priced CDs, shirts, and so on. Give your customers a pricing choice. Not everyone will have the available cash for a CD or higher-end shirt. Selling lower-priced items allows those people to take something home, while you make a little bit of dough. A little bit of something is loads better than a lot of nothing.

You might be one of the lucky ones who have a band member with some design talent. The Beatles did. John Lennon attended art school. KISS's lead guitarist, Ace Frehley, designed the band's iconic logo, Davie Bowie was a graphic designer before he morphed into Ziggy Stardust.

But before you start designing, give careful thought to product. What can you successfully sell? CDs, of course—they're a staple. As mentioned, wearables are a big item. As a matter of fact, T-shirts, in particular, can account for as much as 80 percent of your merch sales. Eighty percent! Look at your fans. What are they wearing? T-shirts? Hats? Bracelets? Here are a few ideas to help get you started:

- CDs
- USB drives (branded with your logo and containing an original song or two)
- T-shirts, tanks, polo shirts, sweatshirts, and hoodies
- Hats and caps
- Drink ware: mugs, water bottles, sippy cups, and shot glasses
- Bags: tote bags, gym bags, and shoulder bags
- Jewelry: logo necklaces and bracelets
- Keychains
- Posters
- Bumper stickers, buttons, and badges
- iPhone and iPad cases and laptop and Kindle skins and sleeves

The product possibilities are practically endless. If you can print your logo on it, you can sell it. If you can also print your site address on it, so much the better. The more products you offer, the more sales you'll generate, and, ultimately, the more money you'll earn.

Don't forget the "up-sell." The up-sell is selling additional products to the same customer, usually ones that complement the original sale. It's anybody's guess how much additional revenue McDonald's brings in with the simple added line, "Would you like fries with that?" Use the same technique. When a fan, aka a customer, buys a shirt, offer the person a hat to go with it. If the customer buys a keychain, how about a USB drive to hang on it?

To ensure that up-sell systems work, you'll need to train your people at the table. Sure, some will forget to ask customers about additional items at first. But over time, the up-sell can bring quite a bit of additional revenue.

PRODUCTION NEEDS

Going the traditional route will require tapping into the services of others. That usually means a graphic designer, screen and/or offset printer, CD/USB drive duplication service, and, perhaps, some others, depending on your product line.

The Graphic Designer

A graphic designer, if you don't already have one, is needed to create your saleable designs, prepare artwork for screen or offset printing, and also guide you through the process, make recommendations, and provide options and ideas. Check with friends, family, and pretty much everybody you've ever met in your life for references and referrals. Always check out designers' portfolios, on- or offline. Ideally, find somebody with a good reputation who's done this type of work before. Not all graphic designers excel or are even familiar with certain reproduction methods. Most, or at least the good ones, are often specialists in a certain type of work, such as brochures, annual reports, websites, publications, logos, and so on. There are also those who specialize in band and artist materials, along with merchandise design and production.

Although I've never used it, you might try an outfit called BandJob. com. From its site: "Band Job is dedicated to the role of visual arts in music. A place created for professional designers working within the music industry to showcase their work and shoot the s—— with fellow artists." By the way, BandJob allows cursing on their site forum. I like that. It makes things a bit more "real." How refreshing.

BandJob.com isn't a contest or crowdsourcing site. Those are sites where hundreds, if not thousands, of "designers," several of whom might be 11-year-old kids with a bootleg copy of Adobe Creative Suite, submit designs and hope to win a gig. These projects are the buck-and-a-quarter type of job with little, if any, input from the "client." Beyond that, sadly, artwork is often ripped off from authentic designers or isn't up to production standards. Sometimes designs are slightly modified, but it's still a potential, if not outright, copyright infringement. You don't want to get sued over your logo or product art. Turn and run from these places.

If I understand things correctly, you can purchase completed designs found on BandJob from the designer or contact the designer for something that's more custom-made. The latter is a good idea. Inasmuch as you don't need a copyright suit headache, you don't want to have another act with the same artwork. That's just plain ol' beyond embarrassing, especially if you both end up playing at the same venue.

When discussing products with your designer, ensure that your final decisions align with your branding. That means the logo is consistent in its structure, colors match your logo and other branding efforts, typography is the same, and so on. You get the idea. Now might be a good time to go back and review chapter 3 about branding and marketing.

In conventional printing, color costs money. That means your stunning, four-color logo is going to cost more to print than a one- or two-color version. Your designer can create those different color options for you. Ideally, have your logo in black and white (one color), a two-color version, and a multicolor version. You might find it wise to spring for a multicolor shirt, but only go with one color for a keychain or USB drive. Talk these options over with your designer, and ask the designer to get quotes for you from a few printers. Ideally, get at least three quotes and ensure they're "apples to apples," not "apples to oranges."

Also, many products have a specific design placement area and sometimes more than one. For example, some shirts allow for printing on the chest, back, and sleeve areas. Others allow only for printing on the front and in a certain size. These are yet more topics to discuss with your designer. And here you thought all designers did was create nifty artwork. These folks can save you a lot of dough and your hindquarters. Be open with them. Discuss various options and ideas. They're worth their weight in salt. I'm not just writing that because I come from a design background. Well . . . OK, I sort of am. But, nonetheless, it's true.

As is my custom, here's another little bit of fairly useless trivia to know, tell, and amaze your friends. "Worth their weight in salt" originates from the Middle Ages, when salt was rare and valuable and from the Roman Empire. A person who was "worth their weight" was, and still is, a person who is needed and valuable. Roman soldiers were allowed a certain amount of money to buy salt. These guys had to buy their own food, weapons and such. The cost of these goods were deducted from their wages, in advance. How much does that suck? Plus, the word "salary" is based on the Latin word "sal," which means salt. The complete word, for those who are interested, is "salarium." Roman soldiers received a salarium. I wonder if they were also paid overtime or received a bonus based on the number of disembodied body parts achieved during battles?

Printing and Reproduction

A decent graphic design will lighten your wallet a bit. Printing and reproduction costs can clean it out, if you're not careful. As mentioned, give thought to how many colors should appear on which products. Get at least three quotes for each product. By the way, you don't need to create an entire product line from the get-go. Start with a few products and build from there. Sure, you'll need CDs and T-shirts to start, but other wearables, mugs, keychains, and such can come later.

As with a graphic designer, start by asking around for referrals. Check with other bands to learn where they had their merch made and how the experience was for them. Also check the Big Kahuna, Google. There are loads and loads of online sources for merchandise production. Often costs will be lower than using a local shop.

If you get quotes on your own, be as clear and specific as possible. That means communicating the needed quantity, number of colors used in the design, product colors and sizes, taxes, and delivery options, as well as delivery fees. Be aware that there are usually minimum order numbers to be dealt with, setup costs, shipping costs, and possibly other costs. Ensure you know them all. If you don't understand something, ask and continue to ask questions until it's all crystal clear. You don't want to place an order and then get a sky-high surprise invoice. Also, be aware that a quote is a firm price usually good for a specific period of time, such as thirty days. An estimate is more of a nebulous thing, as in, "Well, it's probably going to cost $XYZ." In other words, a quote is cast in stone, while an estimate is a best guess. They're usually pretty darn good guesses, based on historical data, similar projects, and so on, but they can change. If they do, the supplier should notify you in advance—ideally, well in advance.

Finally, you'll need a place to store all your merch in between shows. Odds are, you won't be hauling the entire lot with you for each gig. You or a band mate might have a basement that is watertight as well as relatively temperature- and humidity-controlled. If so, count yourself among the fortunate few. You may need to rent a space, such as a warehousing service, to store your stuff. Don't just cram the merchandise into the trunk of yours and your band members' cars. That would be bad and a sure way to lose a load of dough when Mother Nature doesn't want to play nice and rain ruins your products. Think ahead. This stuff starts to take up space rather quickly.

E-COMMERCE, SELLING ONLINE, AND SELLING ON THE ROAD

There are simple solutions to all the points mentioned earlier. They're CafePress.com and PayPal.com. No doubt, right about now you're cursing my name and wishing me to Hell for making you wade through all the stuff you had to read that preceded this section. (By the way, "Hell" is a (supposed) place and therefore a proper noun, so it should be capitalized. Remember that the next time you shoot off a testy email.)

CafePress.com is a site that makes stuff—stuff you can sell. Most of the items mentioned in the list I included previously are available from CafePress. But here's the really slick part. They, unlike your local screen printer, print on demand. That means if somebody orders one T-shirt, CafePress prints one T-shirt and ships one T-shirt. This is handy. No dealing with printers, minimums, or additional costs such as shipping and storage. CafePress handles all that for you and taxes.

Here's how the site works. You set up an account, pick your products, upload your design that you got from your designer, position it where you want it to appear on the item, and set a selling price. Cafe-Press charges a wholesale price for its products. You mark that up to your selling price. CafePress keeps their wholesale amount. You make the markup. For example, a standard T-shirt from CafePress costs on the order of $15.99. You might mark that up $10 to $25.99. You make the $10, and CafePress makes the $15.99. But CafePress also offers a 100 percent guarantee and usually ships in twenty-four hours. You set up how you prefer to be paid. It can be by check or PayPal, and payments are set to go out when the number of products sold, which you set, is reached.

Their products are pretty good, too. Years ago, I created a character called Emo Zioni, applied his numerous emotional expressions to several CafePress products, and set up a CafePress store. A friend of mine bought a hat. He's had it for years. It's been through the washer more times than I can count, and the design still holds up. Sure, it's faded a bit. I need to remind him to go easy on the bleach. But it's held up nonetheless.

The moral of the story is that it might be a better bet to start off with a site such as CafePress in the beginning. You can also buy as many of your own products as you like at their wholesale price. So, let's say you have a small show coming up. You can order and pay for a few dozen

T-shirts and other products from CafePress, at wholesale, and they'll ship them to you. You have enough, or, better, the *right* amount of product for the merch table at the show and you're good to go.

You can also integrate your CafePress store, which is, by the by, "brandable," into your site for online sales. By "brandable," I mean you can add your band or act logo, colors, and similar elements to make the experience as seamless as possible for visitors. Just add a "Store" link in the navigation that points to your CafePress shop—easy.

As you sell more products and orders start to get heavy, you'll probably want to convert your site store over to something more robust. Magento, a free, open-source application, is available with many hosting packages, as is X-Cart and a myriad of others. PayPal also provides a dedicated e-commerce shopping cart. These e-commerce applications provide many more features, such as integration with Quickbooks, list building, and much more. But start off smaller first and grow from there.

If you offer just a few products, you can get away with a couple of simple "Buy Now" PayPal buttons. When it's time to move up, you'll need a few other things. In order to accept credit and debit cards, you'll need an Internet merchant account, which is available from your bank, although difficult to obtain in many cases. Your hosting company can often help you through the process, and it's usually a much easier way to go.

An Internet merchant account is different from a brick-and-mortar merchant account; that's the type used at, for example, a retail store. You'll also need a gateway account. The gateway account is what ties your customer's credit or debit card to your bank account. It's the vehicle to get the moolah from your customer's wallet into your bank account. Your web designer can help you with these accounts and provide you with further information. Getting into full-blown e-commerce solutions is outside the scope of this book.

Should you decide to accept credit cards at your merch table—and you should—PayPal has a great new tool called "Here." It's a credit or debit card reader that plugs into your iPhone or other smartphone. From PayPal's site: "Use your smartphone to securely process card payments with our new plug-in card reader. It's a simple way to accept cards, PayPal, and even checks—anywhere you do business. And unlike other readers, PayPal Here helps protect card information as it's swiped with the highest level of encryption and is highly secure."

The ability to accept credit and debit cards at your merchandise table can greatly increase your revenue. Many people carry little, if any, cash these days. Plastic is just an easier and often safer option. In addition, with plastic, people tend to be a little more impulsive and not think as much about costs as they do with cash.

Getting set up with PayPal is easy and pretty straightforward. If your band or act is officially a business (e.g., a corporation, sub-chapter S, or LLC), and it has a bank account in the band's name, get set up with a PayPal Business account and also get verified by PayPal. Verification increases PayPal's security and also enhances the tie between your bank account and PayPal. It also gives you additional information about your customers. Verification also helps build trust on the customer/fan end.

PROMOTING AND MANNING THE MERCH TABLE AND BEAN COUNTING

Have everybody working the table wear a band shirt. That should be a no-brainer, but it's often overlooked. If you're blessed with roadies, or just some friends helping out with setup and tear-down, have them wear your shirts, too.

Have a cashbox at the table with real cash in it. You're going to need to make change. Have an e-newsletter signup sheet and ensure that you can read the addresses people enter. If possible, get them into a laptop or tablet as quickly as possible. Ask the fan to verify the address, as in, "Is that joe.blow@xyz.com?" Have a poster, or other display item, with a sample of your e-newsletter and some compelling points as to why fans should sign up. A quality printout and decent color copies of a sample newsletter can do the trick as well. Those points might be show dates, merchandise specials for subscribers, band news, and the like. A poster might simply be an oversized printout from an office supply store that's mounted to foam core board with a display easel attached to the back so that it will stand up. Your local office supply store will carry all these items, and many stores will handle the mounting for a small additional fee.

Get a table skirt with your logo on it and, if you have some extra money you don't know what to do with, also a back wall and/or vertical banners that will make the table much more visible. FedEx/Kinkos (or whatever they're calling themselves these days) or a similar office supply store can help get your materials produced at a fairly reasonable rate. But shop around. Even "reasonable rate" can mean expensive.

If you can afford it, check out trade show suppliers, via an Internet search, for display items. Skyline Displays (www.skyline.com) is a great company, and I've used them often for my clients' tradeshow displays. Back walls and banners can have band images, logos, and other elements that will help engage your fans. Action images are often better than static band photos. Again, if you can afford it, have some professional images shot at live shows, specifically for use on your merch table display materials. Professional-level table display materials will give your act a polished look. That can also go a long way toward drawing fans to the table and getting them to dig deep into their pockets.

Fortunately, these display items are usually a one-time expense, especially if you take good care of them. That means not eating or drinking stuff at the merch table. Have a card table in the back for that kind of thing. Be sure to fold table skirts and such nicely, and store them with great care. If you do, they'll last a long time, and you'll certainly get your money's worth from them.

Another good option is to create merchandise bundle packages. That might mean a shirt and hat combination at a discounted rate, or a CD and T-shirt combo, or maybe a less expensive bumper sticker, keychain, and USB drive with tunes package. You're creative. Get some ideas going.

Here's a word to the wise: Maybe it's because I'm a cynical old guy who has no faith in humankind, or it might be the places I've lived. . . . But people steal stuff. Yeah, I know it's hard to believe, but true nonetheless. At some point (hopefully not several), somebody is going to try their best to lift some merch from you. To avoid this faux pas, have your merchandise on display on the table or on boards behind it, but keep the real saleable stuff either under the table or behind it. In other words, keep the bulk of your merchandise where nobody is going to get a five-finger discount at your expense.

Bean Counting

To see if you're really making money or not, you'll need a system in place. It can be a simple paper ledger, but a spreadsheet is better. Your spreadsheet should have each product listed, along with its price, the venue name where it was sold, the number of units sold, whether it was a cash or credit card sale, size, color, other specs, and, of course, the total amount sold at the event. Over time, you'll learn what sells best and what doesn't. It can take some time to set up the spreadsheet, but it's well worth the effort. It will give you the information you need to tighten up your product offerings or ordering, in terms of the type of product, colors, sizes, and so on. Having a laptop or tablet at the table will make this a snap. A snap, that is, as long as the people manning the table remember to enter the information.

After each show, or at least each month, look over your numbers. Make product adjustments as needed. Buy more of what sells and dump the dogs. It's just plain economics. Give the people what they want. When you do, they'll come back for more and tell people about your show and your stuff. That will increase your fan base, which in turn, over time, means more money in your bank account.

Promote Your Merchandise

In between songs or sets, don't be afraid or ashamed to promote your merchandise. Sure, you want to sing and play your heart out. You also want to make money. Your act, as I've mentioned, is a business. Businesses that thrive promote their products and services. It's called marketing.

Be sure to mention your merch table, where it's located, and what you have to offer. As a matter of fact, mention this information a few times during the show. Say something like, "Hey! Check out our T-shirts. You can find them at the table near the entrance. Shirts are just $25.99, and they're killer! There's also a bunch of other cool stuff out there, including our latest CD, so stop by before you take off. After the show, the band will be there for a meet and greet."

Promote your merchandise on your site as well. Add some banner ads that link to your store with some great graphics and engaging words to tell people why they should visit and buy something.

When the time comes to do a morning radio show interview, bring some doughnuts as I mentioned earlier, but also bring some T-shirts or other merchandise for the radio staff and some to give away on the show—a "Caller Seven will win a band T-shirt" kind of thing. Do the same for any interviews you're invited to do. It's important to keep these people and your fans happy. Happy fans buy stuff like show tickets, CDs, and merchandise and promote your act. Happy radio people play your tunes and also help promote your act. It's all about building quality, authentic relationships.

Finally, don't forget to ask your fans what type of merchandise is important to them. This is one area where an e-newsletter and social media presence really come in handy. Getting feedback from fans will help ensure that you take action based on facts and not guesses. You can create and purchase merchandise with more confidence, knowing that it's actually wanted, and you'll have a much better likelihood of selling more items.

11

Legal Issues and Your Business Team

I've mentioned this several times, and it bears stating again, especially for this chapter. Whether you like it or not, your act, whether solo or a group, is a business. Because you've gotten this far into this book, you've understood that it's more than just being a great player and putting on a good show. It's also about being successful from a business point of view. There are plenty of other resources to help with developing your talent, musical abilities, theory, and so forth.

Establishing your act as a business means acting like a business, tapping into tried-and-true best practices for marketing, promoting, and managing the money and your musical enterprise. It also means becoming "official." You have several options for that. Some might be better than others for your particular situation. Each option offers its own benefits and drawbacks. Making this decision is also going to require the help, advice, and skills of a trusted team of advisors. These include your manager, agent, accountant, attorney, business insurance agent or broker, and your business banker. Just being a good solo act or band isn't enough to ensure success. It takes business savvy and the aid of a group of knowledgeable, experienced professionals whom you can trust.

How to account for income, expenses, taxes, dealing with contracts and copyrights, disputes, risk management, and your act's business checking account, loans, and other financial services has a significant effect on the health and smooth operation of your musical business.

There are lots of small businesses, music-related or otherwise, that go it alone without tapping into the regular advice and help of a lawyer, accountant, insurance agent, or business banker. While they may operate successfully, it's a risky decision, especially when things start becoming more complex and larger paychecks begin rolling in. Having a good team in place will help keep you safe and reach your business goals with fewer headaches and anxiety.

Finding the right professionals is no small matter. You'll be spending a good deal of time with these pros, so invest the time needed for detailed research to find the ones who are the best match for your specific circumstance and needs. Your search should begin with your equipment suppliers, other bands and musicians, and various other musical associates. Ask for recommendations—who they use, if they believe they're good and trustworthy, and similar questions. Start by making a few calls and asking around for referrals. Odds are, one or more names will keep cropping up. These are the professionals you want working with you. Let's take a look at each profession, how the professionals can help you, and what you can expect.

The idea is to find professionals who are already familiar with the specifics of the music industry. Just because your parents or friends use a certain attorney, for example, doesn't mean that attorney will be good for you. Odds are, that person won't be. A general practice accountant or lawyer may be perfect for others, but that person probably doesn't know how the music business works. It can hurt you significantly more than help you if a lawyer gives you advice that's off-base. Finding attorneys who understand the business helps ensure that you won't need to train your team of advisors about the business nuances of the music industry. Plus, you probably won't even know the nuances, at least in the beginning. That's why you need the right advisors.

LEGAL STRUCTURES

Let's start off with your legal entity. As mentioned, there are several legal structures, including sole proprietorship, partnership, corporation, and the newer limited liability company, or LLC. Corporations are further divided into C corporations and S corporations.

On the upside, sole proprietorships are easy to set up and a common legal structure for many small businesses, particularly for independent professionals and solo artists. They give the owner complete control over the business. On the downside, this structure exposes the owner to more risk. Sole proprietors are personally liable for all financial obligations of the business. Nonetheless, many bands and, of course, solo acts go this route. After their business begins to grow, they may change to a different structure. Also, be sure to check with your state's secretary of state office to see if you need to register a fictitious name. (In some areas this may be the county clerk's office.) In your case, the fictitious name is the band name. In the case of a solo act who does business under a name that's different from the artist's, the same applies.

Next up is the partnership. A partnership joins two or more people who agree to share in the profits or losses of a business as well as the decision making. Profits are passed through to each partner, who reports them on his or her individual tax returns. On the tax front, the partners file partnership tax returns and adjust their personal returns (1040s) to reflect the profit or losses of the partnership. As in sole proprietorships, each general partner is responsible for the financial obligations of the business. That means that if you form a band partnership, every member is responsible for the financial obligations incurred by the band. So, if your drummer goes off and buys a new kit on credit under the band's name, each member is responsible for that debt.

Partnerships can be general or limited, and many bands opt for this structure. In many ways, a partnership is exactly like a marriage. I don't mean that in a metaphoric way. I mean it literally. Yet it's probably the most common legal structure for bands in which each member is active.

A partnership doesn't need too much in the way of legal stuff, either. A handshake can do the trick. If there's no formal paperwork and two or more people are doing business together, the business is automatically classified as a partnership. And therein lies a large part of, what I believe, is the problem with partnerships. They can be rather fuzzy when it comes to the details, unless there is a rock-solid and clearly drafted formal partnership agreement.

In a general partnership, typically one or more general partners are responsible for the total liabilities and actions of the partnership as well as management authority. So, each general partner is responsible for the actions of the other general partners. This includes not just the business's assets, but the partners' personal assets as well, should legal action be taken against the partnership. This is the main drawback to this type of structure.

In a limited partnership, the limited partners are liable only to the extent of their investment in the company, or band in this case. The downside is that a limited partner has no managerial authority. Managerial authority is generally granted to one general partner.

A partnership, mostly because of the name, sounds like a peachy structure for a band. Maybe so. Maybe no. Get your attorney involved to make recommendations and to draft an agreement. If a band member leaves, for example, the partnership might evaporate. Usually it does. A well-thought-out and clearly defined agreement can cover contingencies and matters that you may think will never happen. Those kinds of things do, in fact, happen and can easily screw up everything you've worked so hard to achieve.

A band operating under a partnership as its legal structure is different from a band partnership agreement (BPA) for the members of the group. A BPA addresses various issues within the band, including who owns the band's name, what happens if a member quits or is fired, how the money is distributed, and how decisions are made. It can also address subjects such as how decisions are made regarding which gigs to play, how equipment is purchased, how internal disputed are handled, and how set lists are decided. BPAs can also address many other operational and structural topics, but they aren't a formal legal partnership agreement that forms the band's legal entity. Essentially, a partnership agreement addresses the band's formal legal structure. A BPA addresses its internal management and administration issues and practices. The BPA can be thought of as a type of operations manual that can lessen or eliminate conflict down the road.

A C corporation is a legal entity that is created to conduct business. In many ways, it's like creating another person. It can be taxed, separate from its founders and shareholders. It can be held legally responsible and liable for its actions. Naturally, it can also make a profit. The primary benefit to having a corporation structure is the ability to avoid personal liability. But corporations also require much more recordkeeping. S corporations are a variation on the "C" variety and, similar to partnerships, allow profit or losses to be passed through, in the form of dividends, on individual tax returns.

A popular new hybrid is the limited liability company (LLC). It can be an excellent choice for bands in many ways. An LLC combines the best parts of the corporate and partnership structures. It provides limited personal liability for the members, like a corporation, while providing much of the flexibility a partnership enjoys. There can often be tax benefits with an LLC, and it has the advantage of profits being passed through to the members. Although a lawyer is required to set up one, the cost to do so is usually less than it is for a C corporation. Like a corporation, though, there is typically more paperwork and documentation involved once the structure has been set up.

MANAGERS AND AGENTS

Defining the difference between a manager and an agent can be a can of worms because of the potential for functional crossover between the positions. In other words, they can, at times, do the same things.

A manager is, arguably, the most important advisor on your team. It's this person's job to direct and guide the overall development of the act. From deciding what you'll wear and play on stage to choosing a producer for a recording, hiring a photographer for a shoot, giving advice about your best bets for attorneys, accountants, and other advisors, and pretty much everything in between, your manager is something like the act's parent. The manager provides advice, guidance, suggestions, and direction to help your act grow, expand, and evolve into the money-making machine it's meant to be. Managers want nothing more than to see your act or band develop into a massive money-making machine because they're typically paid on commission, usually between 10 to 20 percent of overall earnings. That means everything—CDs, live shows, merchandise, and so on—the whole ball of wax.

Given the extensive weight of the manager's input and his or her effect on an act's success or failure, you don't want to muff up your choice of manager. This is a person you need to trust with your life, because you do, in so many ways. We've all read the horror stories of bad management, of acts being robbed blind. Seek out an experienced professional with a great reputation for getting things done, making excellent decisions, and being utterly honest. Utterly honest, by the way, isn't just about business deals. Your manager should be a person who will tell you when a tune is good, but, perhaps more important, when a tune is no good, when a band member is off, and similar things you need to hear but may not particularly want or like to hear.

Never, under any circumstance, agree to hire a manager based on a handshake deal. While that might be very polite, if you do, you might as well bend over in the process. Always have a written contract that's been drafted by your attorney and preferably signed in blood. The contract, or agreement, should address the length of the agreement (how long the manager will be with you); the manager's responsibilities; what those responsibilities are, specifically; the amount of compensation (commission); whether or not the manager will be paid for his or her expenses; what authorization the manager has to make communications on behalf of the band without prior approval; specific milestones, both short- and long-term (what you can expect to be done and by when); and when and under what circumstances contract termination is acceptable.

AGENTS

Agents are the folks who get your act booked. They're the gig-getters, and they usually snag the kind of gigs you wouldn't have a snowball's chance in Hell of booking on your own. So, in many ways, they're also worth their weight in salt, like a great manager. Also like finding the right manager, shop around to find an agent who is a good fit for your band or solo act. Is the person with a huge booking agency? If so, you may not get the attention you need. Conversely, if the agent is too small in scope or unknown, he or she probably won't be in a position to book you into some excellent venues.

Agents are paid by the show. In other words, they book you into this venue or that and they make a commission, usually 10 percent off the top of those shows. They don't make money off your merchandise, record sales, songwriting royalties, or other revenue sources; they just profit from the gigs they book. There will be a contract involved. Have your attorney look it over with care. Never agree to any commissions or fees beyond bookings. Also, try your best to keep contract terms down to one year, if possible. Unless you happen to be a gifted clairvoyant, you can't see into the future and learn what this person will do for you. You can usually renew and renegotiate near the end of the contract's term.

Finally, when it comes to agents and touring outside of the country, try to get an agent in the local market you plan to visit. That agent will be much more familiar with the lay of the land. Ensure that this is in your contract with your main agent. Also, ensure that if you aren't booked within a specified period of time, the deal's off. That's normally ninety days, give or take.

ACCOUNTANTS

Number crunchers come in a few flavors. These include book-keepers, accountants, and certified public accountants (CPAs). The one that's right for you, like so many things in business, depends. The critical factor is that you get the right help in setting up and implementing the financial systems for your band.

Bookkeepers do just that—they keep the books, otherwise known as your financial records. They record income and expenses for your act, also known as "money in and money out." They may also handle sales tax recordkeeping and other types of financial notation. They may or may not have an accounting degree. As such, their services are usually limited to the tedious task of data entry. For example, small businesses with employees often employ a full- or part-time bookkeeper who manages the day-to-day financial entries, along with running various reports and payroll duties. But many bookkeepers are freelancers, and you can tap into their services on an as-needed basis. A good freelancer with an excellent reputation might be just the ticket for your band (pun intended). Depending on how many numbers your band or solo act needs to enter, that can mean weekly or monthly bookkeeping. Also, some bookkeepers are certified by accounting software such as Quick-Books and MYOB. If you're set up with either of those programs, it can be a good idea to find a certified bookkeeper.

Accountants have been educated in accounting practices and will often have a bachelor's degree in either accounting or business. They may even have a master's degree. They fall between the skill sets of book-keepers and CPAs. It's important to note that not all accountants possess bookkeeping skills or are skilled in various accounting software. It may be hard to believe, but there are still diehards out there who do their work with a pencil and paper. Considering this, be sure to ask if an accountant is familiar with the software you use and discern the person's comfort level with it.

The certified public accountant (CPA) is what most small business owners think of when it comes to accountants and is likely the best bet for a successful band or even one starting on its way up. CPAs have completed college business and accounting coursework and possess a degree. In addition, they have completed well over 100 hours of business courses specifically for CPAs. Beyond this, they will have worked for at least one year under the supervision of a CPA before being eligible to take the CPA exam and obtain a license. Needless to say, a professional who has gone through this process has some valuable knowledge. With that knowledge comes a price tag, and you can expect to pay more for the services of a CPA than for a regular accountant, and certainly more than for a bookkeeper.

Your accountant can provide a variety of services to help keep your musical enterprise safe, profitable, and growing. Some of these include

- Designing and setting up your accounting system
- Preparing, clarifying, and reviewing financial statements and reports
- Performing various financial calculations and projections
- Aiding you in drafting the financial section of your business plan
- Providing advice for major purchases, such as equipment, sound boards, and the generally expensive stuff
- Providing tax planning and strategies
- Preparing tax returns
- Helping you obtain loans
- Providing detailed financial advice for your business

One question that will arise in your search for the right accountant is whether to hire a large firm, small firm, or independent person. Large national or regional firms will offer the most services and have the most experience in specialized financial areas, such as the music industry. They can also provide a credibility shot in the arm for a band or independent performer. When bankers, lenders, or even managers, agents, and producers learn that you're aligned with a well-known firm, they may take you a bit more seriously than the group who uses a member's self-employed uncle as their accountant.

The downside of using a Hugeo, Mondo and Bigg CPA is that you may not get the personal attention you need, or you may have your account assigned to a first-year accountant who may not do the best job for you. Conversely, working with a smaller firm or independent will bring more attention to your needs from a senior-level partner or owner, while usually being less costly.

Another factor is how you plan to work with your accountant. Do you envision a very tight relationship, where you meet at least once each month, or will you only see this person at tax time? Are you seeking general advice for tax planning and financial matters, or do you need detailed advice and help on a regular basis? There are no right or wrong answers, but having a clear idea of how you will use an accountant's services will greatly help you in choosing the right one. Beyond this, it's important to find one who is a good match for your personality and, like the rest of your team, understands the industry and has some experience with it. This person may not become your best friend, but you should at least like him or her.

ATTORNEYS

Like your accountant, your attorney is destined to become one of your best business friends and can be integral to the success and safety of your musical business. But many small business owners, as well as musicians, have a problem when it comes to attorneys: They don't hire a lawyer until they need one to fix whatever problem has reared its ugly head. Finding a lawyer who's a good fit for your business and building a relationship with this person before you need him or her to fix problems is wise.

Like your other business advisors, begin by asking trusted friends, other bands, equipment suppliers, and similar associates for referrals and recommendations. Finding an attorney with entertainment industry experience and, ideally, knowledge of music-related legal issues will help ensure that his or her advice is on target.

Although it can be tempting and seem easier to use your personal lawyer, it's most likely not the best idea. This person might be a friend but may lack the specific skills and knowledge required by a music- and entertainment-oriented business. It's important to evaluate whether your problem, whatever it might be, needs a specialist or can be handled by a lawyer with a general practice. For example, suppose you haven't been paid for a gig that you successfully played. Any lawyer with a general practice should be able to handle this for you. But what if you've been offered a record label deal for a CD recording or three? Here you'd be wise to find a lawyer with a special understanding of entertainment law and its subtleties. In essence, your legal provider should be a tight fit for your potential legal challenges and needs within the field of music and entertainment. Your lawyer should also be able to refer you to other attorneys for specific needs and challenges, such as trademark registration for your band logo, registration for the act's name, and such. (Which, by the way, you should have for both your logo design and your band's name. The logo can get by with a ™, and the band name gets a ® after it's registered with the government's Patent and Trademark Office.)

As mentioned, obtain referrals from business and music associates, family, and friends. If you've already started working with some other business advisors, be sure to ask them, too. Your business advisors should be well connected within your community and able to provide a few names.

With your list in hand, visit potential attorneys' websites to learn more about them. Also check business social media sites such as LinkedIn and review profiles. Check with your area's Bar Association and also the Martindale-Hubbell Law Directory, which can be accessed online at Lawyers.com. The directory provides brief bios and information about experience and specialties. Many listed attorneys are rated by confidential opinions gathered from other lawyers and judges. Also check into any disciplinary action taken against the candidates. Most lawyers are licensed in a single state, but some are licensed in more than one. Begin by checking with the American Bar Association online at abanet.org. The site lists each state's disciplinary agency.

From your research, create a short list of good prospects and make an appointment to meet. This isn't the time for idle chitchat. You're on a mission to find the best lawyer for your business. Here are some key questions to ask:

- How many clients do you have in my industry?
- What is your experience in legal matters for musicians?

- What are some of the challenges I can expect while operating my band or solo act?
- Are there others in the firm who would work on my account, or will it only be you?
- How will I be billed, and what are some typical charges?
- How do you handle client communications? Meetings? Email? Phone?
- How accessible can I expect you to be?
- Are you currently handling any of my competitors?

Your final decision will be based on your research, the personal interview, and also your gut feeling. Gut feelings may not sound very scientific, but they're often correct. If an attorney does not sit well with you, even if that person gave you all the right answers, there's usually a reason. Your attorney will be privy to very personal information about you and your band. As such, trust is imperative. A certain lawyer may come with stellar testimonials, a spotless background check, and graceful words, but none of that means anything for you if you don't feel you can trust that person totally.

What can your attorney do for you? Here are some highlights:

- Help you develop your business plan
- Draft and review contracts, letters of agreement, and other legal documents
- Help settle client, venue, or supplier disputes
- Collect past due fees
- Negotiate contracts
- Help get you out of a bad deal
- Draft and review licensing agreements
- Educate and help you with copyright issues, including infringements, filing forms, and negotiating usage rights
- Be your litigation advisor and advocate
- Offer advice on your legal problems by telling you what to do or not to do

- Help to settle disputes for you out of court, saving you time, headaches, and expense
- Represent you in the civil courts

INSURANCE AGENT OR BROKER

Unless you're independently wealthy, and even if you are, you're going to need some form of insurance to thwart the business risks. Equipment gets stolen, vehicles get into accidents, and there are music-industry-specific risks, such as special event liability insurance, borrowed equipment insurance, life and health insurance, and so on. You need to protect your assets.

There are a myriad of insurance products available today that are sold by either an agent or a broker. An agent represents a specific insurance company and sells only its products. A broker, on the other hand, represents several companies. Plus, a broker often offers advice and recommendations from a more objective point of view in exchange for a commission on the sale. In addition, this person can act as your advisor, advocate, and intermediary when a claim needs to be handled. The majority of insurance brokers are also small business owners, so they may be more sensitive to the needs and circumstances of a band or solo performer because you're both small businesses.

Both agents and brokers can guide you through the insurance maze. They can also help you develop a risk management strategy with a mix of products and special coverage. Some questions to ask when choosing an agent or broker are the following: Does this person have the right experience for your needs? You may be tempted to use your personal insurance agent for your band, but that person may not have the proper background and experience to offer the best coverage. Beyond liability, can your agent or broker offer you a comprehensive package that will also protect your business assets? Can you trust this person to provide you with sound advice?

Your relationship with your agent or broker should be more than simply buying a policy. If a particular person seems more interested in his or her commission, you might want to try someone else. Your insurance person should be part of your team, not simply someone you see only when there's a problem.

BUSINESS BANKER

One of the first things you'll do when launching your "official" band business is open a business checking account. Here's what usually happens. Let's say the band is a sole proprietorship. A band leader does a little research, checks some ads and websites, and settles on a bank that looks just right. The leader strolls in and sits down with a banker. After exchanging a few pleasantries, the banker has the band member fill out some forms, choose a check design and processes the musician's first deposit. They shake hands, and the business owner leaves. That's often the end of the relationship. Many small business owners, as well as musicians, are on a first-name basis with the bank's tellers but don't have a clue about the bankers.

Finding the right bank involves many factors, and one of the first questions on your mind will be "Should I use a large national or regional bank or a small local one?" If easy access to ATMs and branch locations is important to you, a large bank may be the right choice. These banks typically have numerous branch offices in a city or town and are members of common ATM networks. That can mean you'll save money on ATM fees. This can be important if you tour often. But individual service may suffer, and the bank may not focus on small and micro-businesses, such as a solo artist or band.

Smaller banks are often better at customer service, and small businesses may be a large part of their customer base. But they probably don't offer as many locations, and you may find yourself paying ATM fees on a regular basis. Smaller banks might not offer the breadth of services that their larger cousins can. Virtually all banks offer online services. If you find one that doesn't, you might want to look elsewhere. When it comes to lending, large banks often have many layers in the review process. That means getting a yes or no will take more time. Smaller banks tend to be more nimble in their review process.

Beyond your checking account, there are several things a business banker can do to help your business, so building a quality relationship with this person can be important. But it can also be tricky. Unlike your attorney, who makes money by keeping you safe, or your accountant, who makes money by saving you some, bankers are largely profit-driven through lending and selling products and services. As such, they want you to be successful, so you'll use more of their services and obtain loans and other forms of credit.

A good banker has seen many businesses come and go. The banker has learned what works and what doesn't work. That experience can be of great value to you. If you're lucky and the banker works with a few musicians, he or she may also be in a good position to discuss industry and small-business trends that may affect your operations. Your banker can also be an excellent referral and networking resource. A close relationship with your banker can mean he or she will go to bat for you to help you get better rates or alert you before potential problems become big headaches.

Your banker can help you obtain a line of credit or loan. A common saying, though, is that banks are happy to lend money to people who don't need it. To a large degree, that's true. They want to see an impeccable credit history and sound ability to repay the loan. So, it can be a good idea to arrange a personal line of credit or small loan before you need one—as in, while you have a full-time job and haven't gone full-time musician yet. Repay it swiftly and establish your business with the bank. Having credit established with your bank can save you from scrambling when the unexpected happens and you need to tap into a line of credit or loan quickly.

Nonetheless, when it comes to loans and creative enterprises, bankers tend to act like . . . well, bankers. When you waltz in seeking a loan for band equipment, wait a bit after your banker laughs his toupee off and gets up off the floor. He may listen to you if you've been a good customer and have established excellent credit with his employer. But, in reality, he's still probably going to laugh his pudgy head off. Bankers tend to scoff at creative enterprises seeking loans and lines of credit. If you give it a try, though, be well-prepared with hard documentation of payment histories, financials from your accountant, and anything else that might help your case.

ALTERNATE SOURCES OF CAPITAL

There is another way to get some dough for equipment, touring expenses, recording, and marketing. It's a relatively new phenomenon called fan-funding, a first cousin to crowdfunding. Fan-funding is music that is funded directly by the fans of an artist. In simpler terms, your fans give you the money you need to entertain them.

Most fan-funding takes place online. Some of the sites are Artist-Share.com, Aucadia.com, PledgeMusic.com, and, the most popular and well known of them all, Kickstarter.com. Kickstarter.com isn't any small potato. They've helped raise millions for various creative projects, including music and recording. Their most recent PR coup was capturing funding for the Pebble. Pebble is a watch that connects with a person's smartphone, such as an iPhone or Android. The product does a lot of stuff, such as email notifications, messaging, calendars, and so on, and uses apps to do it. Through Kickstarter.com, Pebble raised over $10 million from just under 70,000 backers in less than thirty-seven days. Not too shabby. Not too shabby at all.

Use Your Team

In closing, your team of business advisors can and likely will become one of your biggest business assets. They're as important as having reliable amps and state-of-the-art recording software. Choose them with the utmost care. You'll be spending a lot of time with them and sharing the most intimate details about your band and yourself with them. Your team can provide objective insights from outside your musical enterprise. These are often insights you'd never have yourself. A musician and small business owner is often too close to his or her music and can't always see the forest for the trees.

Although many small businesses meet with their individual advisors on a regular basis, they don't usually bring all of them together at the same time. You might consider holding a meeting, at least annually, attended by all your advisors. Getting everybody together can be a springboard for new ideas and help grow your band or act faster and with more stability.

WHEN A&R COMES CALLING

Most of the time it will be your marketing and promotional efforts that attract an A&R scout. But at times, the scout may hear about your act through various associates or be at an event to listen to a certain band and also hear yours and like what he or she hears. However it happens, when A&R comes calling, it's critical to be prepared if you hope to get signed.

In many ways, a record label is like a lender. If you get signed, as mentioned earlier in this book, the label machine kicks into gear. The label develops your act, arranges and finances recordings, promotes artists, manages and directs publicity, and manages legal issues, distribution, and all the other tasks involved in getting music into the end customers' hands. All this costs money and lots of it. So, in many ways, the label is taking a big risk when it signs your act. Can you and your music generate enough revenue so that the label, at bare minimum, breaks even? Breaking even, though, isn't going to get you too far. The label is gambling that you're the one who will connect with the fans, draw them in and make a ton of cash, much of which will go to the label to cover costs and ensure its profit margin.

Before the label takes the big gamble, like a lender, it's going to want to know a lot about you and your act, your fan base, and additional resources or services you can bring to the table, such as songwriting, arranging, or even graphic design and other creative services. The more valuable you can make yourself and the more dough you can save the label, the better your chances of striking a deal and signing a contract.

Here are a few tips and "must-haves" to ensure that you're ready when the A&R folks and the label find you:

- You are very motivated to succeed, are professional, appear to be easy to work with, and are likeable to the label and music industry folks and active and potential fans.
- You can demonstrate that you and your band mates have a "we'll do anything" attitude. This may sound like hopping into bed with the Devil. We are talking about the music industry, now aren't we? Labels want to know that the people they sign are committed to the process and aren't going to be prima donna pains in the hindquarters.
- There aren't any substance abuse issues. This is important. An act with substance abuse issues typically costs the label more money in the not-too-long run. The label may find that you're not worth the risk.
- You have a loyal fan base of several hundred. Ideally these are the "evangelist" types who buy whatever you sell, attend your live shows, and generally think your act is the next best thing to sliced bread. If you have an email list that is even broader, so much the better. The label will recognize that these types of fans can be replicated and grown into a much larger group by giving your act more exposure.
- You play a good number of live shows on a regular basis to new audiences.
- Your act has multiple streams of revenue. This means CDs sales but also live shows, merchandise, and other revenue sources, such as songwriting. The labels will know they can capitalize on this quickly.
- You've demonstrated that you understand the importance of marketing and promotion and know how it works. You can show your Facebook page, website, e-newsletter, MySpace page, Twitter feed, press kit, and other public relations materials.

- You can demonstrate a fairly clear understanding of the industry. Perhaps you have recorded and have gained insight into the production process, and you know what a 360 deal is all about. This is part of being professional, but, also, the less the label needs to train you and your band members, the better. Ultimately, the label will save money.

When the time comes to start talking about a contract, don't start bouncing off the walls, agreeing to whatever the label presents. That's just bad business. Always run every contract, whether it's for a record label deal or for a vehicle lease, by your legal eagles. It's their job to protect you and ensure you get a fair deal at the end of the day.

12

Protecting Your Work

As a creative enterprise, you have certain assets called intellectual property. These typically include your logo, the name of your band or solo act, custom graphics used in your branding efforts, and, of course, your songs. All of these intellectual property assets need to be protected. That's usually done through copyrights, along with trademark and name, or "word mark," registration. As an example, your act name and logo are typically protected by registering with the U.S. Patent and Trademark Office, while music and lyrics are protected by registering with the Copyright Office.

I discussed band and act names in chapter 2, but a refresher is probably a good idea. Before settling on a name, do some research to ensure it's not already being used. Google is a good place to start, but you'll also want to check with other organizations and databases such as

- Band Register (www.bandname.com)
- Licensing organizations, including BMI (www.bmi.com) and ASCAP (www.ascap.com)
- U.S. Patent and Trademark Office (www.uspto.gov) using TESS (Trademark Electronic Search System)

Band names can, and should be, registered with the U.S. Patent and Trademark Office. The logo design and band name can be trademarked and use ™ within the logo design or word marked. For example, "Madonna" is a registered word mark, as is "Paul McCartney." The idea behind these marks is ready identification for the public.

Rights in a band name aren't usually created by trade, word, or service mark registration. They're established by use. That means performing and promoting under the name, selling merchandise that carries the name, and so on. So, it's important to keep good records as mentioned in chapter 10.

Trademark registration is another area where it's a good idea to consult with your attorney. It's not required, but a wise move, nonetheless. The registration process, infringement issues, and the like tend to get quite complex and, thus, are out of the scope of this book. I'm not an attorney, so all I can do is touch on the topics. Your attorney can direct you along the correct path and aid in the registration filing process. In addition to any attorney fees, if you choose to use one, the trademark registration fee is roughly $325 at the time of this writing.

UNDERSTANDING COPYRIGHT

Copyright is a collection of exclusive rights granted to the creator of an original work that includes the right to copy, distribute, and adapt the work. These works, however, must be fixed in a tangible medium. For example, a choreographic work might be copyrightable if it's recorded but not if it exists only in the mind of the choreographer. For a musician, that can mean the idea for a song can't be copyrighted, but the song may be copyrighted when it's written down in physical form and also when it's recorded. Ideas are not copyrightable, but the tangible and fixed expression of an idea is.

Think of copyrights as a pie that you can slice up several different ways. Copyright can be licensed in either an exclusive or a nonexclusive transfer. Exclusive transfers include the following rights:

- The right to copy or reproduce the work in any format, whether digital or analog

- The right to make derivative works (all kinds of adaptations of the work, including translations, revisions, film versions of books, etc.)
- The right to control distribution of new copies of the work
- The right to perform the work publicly
- The right to display the work publicly

When licensing nonexclusive rights, the following distinctions can be made:

- Duration of use
- Geographical area in which use is permitted
- The medium in which use is permitted
- The language in which the use is permitted
- Electronic rights may be specifically granted or withheld

There are a few exceptions, known as public interest performances, which can apply under specific circumstances. These include the following:

- Live educational performances
- Transmissions to classrooms
- Religious performances
- Face-to-face performances of musical works for free or for some charitable purpose
- Record stores playing records to promote sales
- Home listening
- Small businesses and restaurants conforming to limitations on the number of loudspeakers and TV screen sizes

Copyright infringement is mostly a civil issue. In other words, if someone infringes on or violates your copyright, you can sue that person. However, there are instances where copyright infringement can be deemed a criminal infringement.

Beginning with the Berne Convention in 1886, efforts have been made to harmonize copyright laws on the international level. However, copyrights remain largely a territorial protection. Each country's laws apply within its borders, but many countries seek to allow some flexibility to address minimum international standards.

Copyrights are potentially very valuable assets. Here's a well-known case in point: In 1985, Michael Jackson bought ATV Music Publishing. ATV owned the rights to roughly 200 songs written by The Beatles' John Lennon and Paul McCartney. Jackson paid $47.5 million for ATV and the Beatles' song rights. In her article "Michael Jackson and the Beatles Copyrights," Renee C. Quinn writes,

> Few people know that Michael Jackson outbid even Paul McCartney himself as well as John Lennon's widow, Yoko Ono, to own the coveted copyrights to The Beatles' music. By owning the copyrights to these timeless songs, Michael earned royalties every time Beatles songs were either played on the radio or performed or sold in stores. While so many are star-struck by musicians and performers, the reality is that the money is in owning the copyrights. Most musicians will never get to the point where they can own their own copyrights free and clear. Record companies lock musicians and performers up in tight, multi-album deals where the ownership of the publishing rights resides with the record label. Only when a musician, band or performer has made it big, fulfilled their multi-album deal and still remains relevant is there much of an opportunity to actually own the lion share of the most lucrative asset in the entertainment business—the publishing rights to the music.[20]

This is one area where a successful indie act or band can really clean up by owning all rights to their music.

In the chapter 9 section "A Word About Copyright," I discuss the Copyright Office, (www.copyright.gov) and how to go about registering musical copyrights. For only $35, registering your work is just plain smart. Plus, as mentioned, you can register several works as a group for the same small fee.

COPYRIGHT AND WORK-FOR-HIRE

Even before a work is formally copyrighted with the Copyright Office, the creator of it owns the copyright. Copyright is vested with the creator on completion of the work. However, it's a good idea to formally copyright your work. In the event of an infringement suit, judgment awards tend to be more favorable for the owner of the copyright who has formally registered it.

The following is from *Copyright Basics*, published by the U.S. Copyright Office: "Copyright protection subsists from the time the work is created in fixed form. The copyright in the work of authorship immediately becomes the property of the author who created the work. Only the author or those deriving their rights through the author can rightfully claim copyright."[21] Also, if you collaborate, the authors of joint works are co-owners of the copyright, unless there is an agreement to the contrary. Ideally, that agreement should be in writing.

Although it's more of an issue for the visual artist or writer, work-for-hire is another potential issue for performing artists, particularly when working in film, video games, or audiovisual applications. The United States Copyright Act of 1976 defines work-for-hire as "(1) a work prepared by an employee within the scope of his or her employment; or (2) a work specially ordered or commissioned for use as a contribution to a collective work, as a part of a motion picture or other audiovisual work, as a translation, as a supplementary work, as a compilation, as an instructional text, as a test, as answer material for a test, or as an atlas, if the parties expressly agree in a written instrument signed by them that the work shall be considered a work made for hire"(17 U.S.C. § 101).[22]

In essence, if you have songwriting or performing clients and sign a work-for-hire agreement, you would be acting as an employee of your client, and rights to the work you create would be vested with the client and not with you.

Several factors are involved in determining whether a person is, in fact, an independent contractor or an employee. To be considered a work-for-hire, all of the following conditions must be met:

The work must come within one of the nine limited categories of works, namely (1) a contribution to a collective work, (2) a part of a motion picture or other audiovisual work, (3) a translation, (4) a supplementary work, (5) a compilation, (6) an instructional text, (7) a test, (8) answer material for a test, (9) an atlas.

The work must be specially ordered or commissioned.

There must be a written agreement between the parties specifying that the work is a work made for hire.

Signing a work-for-hire agreement is never a good idea for an artist, musical or otherwise. If your client presents you with a contract for his or her musical needs, read it carefully to ensure you aren't giving away your rights without adequate compensation. Beyond compensation, if you sign a work-for-hire agreement, you'll also lose the right to use the work in your promotional demo recordings and marketing materials and the rights to use it in or for anything else, such as licensing. Your client will own your work, lock, stock, and barrel.

If a client tries to get you to sign a work-for-hire agreement, it can be at best unethical and at worst illegal. The copyright law doesn't discriminate between ethical and unethical practices. Some unscrupulous companies will knowingly seek to abuse your rights by denying work to those who do not accept work-for-hire. Others will designate work as work-for-hire after the fact by requiring the artist to sign a purchase order or check with work-for-hire terms in the endorsement area. Another shady practice is work-for-hire contracts, understood by the artist to apply only to the current project, but which may actually have language that covers all future work. Be aware that the phrase "work-for-hire" may not be specifically written in the contract, but it could be buried in confusing legalese. When reviewing a contract, look for the following:

- "All rights in all media now in existence or invented in the future in perpetuity throughout the universe"

- Contractual work-for-hire language found in random documents, such as on the backside of paychecks
- Clauses buying all electronic rights
- Multi-year non-compete clauses
- The words "silent partner"
- Clients who claim there was an "implicit" or implied work-for-hire agreement prior to the start of work when none existed
- If the work is deemed not to be work-for-hire, language in the contract that provides for an "all rights" transfer

UNDERSTANDING LICENSING THE RIGHTS PIE

Tied to copyright is the potentially lucrative area of music licensing. To "grant license" simply means to give permission or an authorization. The licensor (you or your representative such as a label, music publishing company, manager, etc.) allows the licensee to use your work under specific circumstances, such as for a specific outlet (film, TV commercial, etc.) for a specified period of time (also called a "term"), in a specific geographic location, and for many other specifics for an agreed sum of money or royalty percentage.

That's pretty much where the simplicity ends when it comes to music licensing. Licensing can become rather confusing, so be sure to consult your attorney for advice.

There are all sorts of opportunities to license your music, and with them come a myriad of usage rights, terms, and definitions. Here are definitions of some of the typical rights used in the music industry:

- Synchronization rights

    These types of rights are used when licensing your music for use in a TV show, movie, commercial ad, radio, and similar media. They're called synchronization rights because your music is synchronized as it's performed, or re-recorded, on the audio recording with the film, commercial, or other medium.

A synchronization royalty is paid to the songwriter and publisher for use as background music.

- Master use rights

    When a potential licensee wants to use a pre-recorded version of your song for a visual project, the licensee must obtain master use rights, in addition to synchronization rights. Master use rights are usually obtained from the record label. But if you're an indie artist, you or your representative may grant them. It's important to note that a master license covers only one tune at a time. So, if someone wants to use every song on one of your albums, that person must purchase a master license for each song.

- Performing rights

    A performance rights license allows a song to be performed either live or via broadcast, such as through radio. Usually, these rights come as a "blanket license," meaning the licensee is granted the right to play a particular Performing Rights Organization's (PRO) entire collection for a set fee. PROs are companies such as BMI and ASCAP. Plays are tracked, and royalties are paid to the writer and publisher.

- Mechanical rights

    A mechanical license is an often-required permission, or license, that allows the licensee to work with, study, improve on, reinterpret, and re-record a song that is protected by copyright. In other words, it's not in the public domain.

    The holder of the license is allowed to create copies of a recorded tune that he or she neither wrote nor have rights of ownership to. Simply put, the copyright holder grants the right to the licensee to reproduce the original recording. Mechanical rights are typically involved when a band records a cover version of a song. It's also required for artists who don't write their own songs but record other songwriters' material. For example, several of the Monkees' (remember them?) songs were written by the songwriting team of Boyce and Hart.

- Grand rights

  When a Broadway producer needs some music to go with a show, grand rights typically come into play. In the United States, PROs do not handle this type of license. It must be negotiated between the copyright owners, publisher, and the production producer.

- Direct license

  A direct license is a form of rights obtained directly from the copyright owner and/or publisher where the performing rights are paid directly to the copyright owner by the licensee. PROs don't enter the picture.

- Downloading royalties

  In music publishing, the fastest growing source of revenue is downloading royalties. When a song or performance is digitally transferred from a source on the Internet or through a mobile device, a royalty is payable. Because most downloading source programs are administered in Western countries, illegal use of copyrights is strictly monitored.

Licensing offers you a variety of benefits, not the least of which is the fact that licenses can be nonexclusive. This means you can license the same song or songs over and over again, to different companies or groups for different purposes. For example, let's say you write a nifty ditty with a great hook. It's catchy, and an ad agency creative director has had the chance to hear it. He decides it would be the perfect background sound-scape for a series of radio and TV spots he's working on. So, you or your representative negotiate a series of licenses that will cover the song's use on the spots (synchronization rights) and the right to use your recording of the song (master rights), and maybe the creative director has a need for an instance where your song will require rerecording for some usage application (mechanical rights). After a while, your mailbox starts to fill up with royalty checks for the variety of usage applications of that single song. Nice!

Then a film producer hears the song on the TV spots and wants to include it in his or her next movie soundtrack—yet another opportunity to license both synchronization and master rights. Plus, your fan base grows when people learn it's your tune and you are playing it. You'll have a credit line in the movie credits, providing you negotiated a good deal. But people can also learn who wrote and performed the song via a Google search, in many cases.

Now, consider licensing several of your works. You may need to buy a bigger mailbox.

For the independent artist, licensing is an effective way to find an entire new audience and grow a fan base. Plus, licensing is an area where the indie artist has a distinct advantage over the big names. Why? Because the big names, their label, and their music publishing company know they're big names and want a load of dough for licensing rights. Unless there's a good reason to spend hundreds of thousands of dollars to license rights from a big-name artist, many potential licensees will opt for a great tune by a lesser-known, and less expensive, artist. Or, they know they can get several songs for the same fee that the big name is demanding for one. Licensing deals with large labels can be a serious hassle, and many companies' music supervisors just don't need the headache.

Music Business and Trend Mongering blog author Mike King is the director of marketing at Berklee Music, and author/instructor of *Music Marketing: Press, Promotion, Distribution, and Retail.* He makes some interesting points in his post "How to Get Your Music in TV and Film." In writing about the live events at the well-known SXSW Conference, Mike notes,

> The overall theme of the panels I attended this year revolved around the ways that artists and music business companies can identify and optimize alternative revenue models as the music business shifts away from traditional record sales. Music licensing,

while nothing new, is a hot topic right now among content owners (songwriters, labels), managers, and artists. Licensing offers the possibility of incredible visibility to artists, and depending on usage, it could also provide a fairly solid revenue stream. . . .

The panelists all agreed that it was a fantastic time for independent artists to look for licensing deals, simply because of economics. Producers are more open to indie music, as A) indie music is typically cheaper to license, and B) many producers consider themselves tastemakers, and want to be known for breaking bands. Alicen Schneider spoke about the fact that 75 percent of the music used by NBC is now independent music. . . .

It's important to also note that when a song is used in TV or film, two licenses are needed: a synchronization license from the copyright owner of the music, as well as [a] master recording license from the copyright owner of the sound recording. These are two separate agreements, and typically, artists that control both their master rights as well as their publishing will do "all in" deals that cover both "sides" of the composition. According to Jennifer from SubPop, artists can expect to receive anywhere from $1,500 to $15,000 for the master rights alone for one-time placements.[23]

That's encouraging news for the artist/songwriter who has the savvy to strike strong licensing deals.

13

The Taxman

It's been said that the only two things in life you can count on are death and taxes. Hopefully, death is a long way off, but taxes are always staring us in the face. The most notorious of these are annual income taxes. Each year in the United States, April 15 rears its ugly head and demands that we dig deep into our pockets. The days and weeks before are often wrought with angst and anxiety. But they need not be, with proper planning and some tax strategy.

In addressing taxes, it's best to begin by defining what business income actually is and isn't. And here's a hint: There's more "is" than "isn't." We normally think of cash, checks, and interest. That's true, but Section 61 of the Internal Revenue Code (IRC) addresses "gross income," which is defined as follows: "Except as otherwise provided in this subtitle, gross income means all income from whatever source derived." That's a very broad definition and includes goods, services, and property, among other things. For bands, solo artists, songwriters, and other musicians, income typically involves live performance fees, CD and download sales, merchandise, royalties, and commissions, along with fan-supported funding if you go that route for subsidizing projects.

Gross income also covers the legal doctrine of "constructive receipt." This means that as soon as money, property, or other income is available to you, it's taxable that year, whether you tap into it or not. So, the check you receive for a gig in December and hold off depositing until January in an effort to reduce your annual income isn't going to hold water with the Internal Revenue Service (IRS).

It may be reassuring to some and downright comical to others, but the fun-loving folks at the IRS aren't too picky when it comes to how the income is generated. Illegal income is also subject to tax. So, if you're lousy at marketing your act and find yourself needing to supplement your income by becoming a moonlighting jewel thief, you'd better keep accurate records. Notorious gangster Al Capone wasn't convicted of any of his obvious crimes. He was sent up the river for tax evasion.

If you work and tour internationally, you'll need to report any income from outside the States. The exception to this is that some income may be excluded if you live and work outside the United States for most of the year. Check with your accountant to ensure that you're reporting correctly.

In the "except as otherwise provided" arena, there are a few tax breaks. Although they may incur other taxes, gifts and inheritances are excluded from taxable income. Likewise, tax-free withdrawals aren't counted as income, and neither is return of capital. For example, if you take a loan against a business or personal asset, say, your home studio equipment, the loan proceeds aren't classified as income. Return of capital is simply recouping your money when you sell an asset. For instance, let's say you invest in a friend's business by purchasing $2,000 worth of stock. He's successful, and you later sell your shares for $3,000. Only the gain of $1,000 is subject to tax. The $2,000 is your return of capital.

The legal structure you choose for your business also impacts how it's taxed. Sole proprietors file a personal income tax form, along with a Schedule C and Schedule SE, also called the Self-Employment Tax, which details business income and expenses. Partnership profits are passed through to the partners, who then individually submit a Form 1099 received from the partnership with a Schedule E. They must also file an informational Form 1065 that the IRS uses to determine if the partners are filing correctly. In addition, they must file a Schedule K-1 that breaks down each partner's share of profits or losses.

The newer hybrid limited liability company (LLC) is a bit more complex. Business owners who elect to be treated as a corporation must file either a Form 1120 or 1120S and a Form 8832, Entity Classification Election, and elect to be taxed as a corporation. LLCs are automatically treated as a partnership when there is more than one owner, unless they file to be treated as a corporation.

Standard corporations, also known as C corporations, file a Form 1120 and face the risk of double taxation. Income taxes are paid first at the corporate level. However, corporate income distributed to individuals as dividends are also subject to taxes as personal income. The less formal S corporation is a bit more relaxed in that income is passed through to individual shareholders in a similar fashion as for partnerships. Taxes aren't paid at the corporate level but are passed through and paid on the individual level.

Confused? You're hardly alone. Welcome to the baffled majority. Income taxes are enough to make your head swim in a sea of convoluted tax codes. Tax codes are designed as much for generating revenue for the government as they are for manipulating credits, loopholes, and deductions in an effort to avoid paying too much. Navigating the United States' innumerable-page tax code is well beyond the average scope of the typical musician, or normal human being for that matter, and the main reason why an army of pinstripe-clad, calculator-toting accountants flourish.

Stepping up on a soapbox and discussing why a tax code should be easy to administer, fair to all, and relatively simple, and why the U.S. system is pretty much just the opposite of that, is out of the scope of this book. If you're interested in learning more, just swing by your local bookseller, where you can find shelves stocked with books on the subject.

Also, before I get too deep into this chapter, I'd be remiss if I didn't add that, professionally, I'm a freelance writer, web and graphic designer, and marketing consultant. I'm not an accountant or lawyer. I've been educated in writing, marketing, art, and design and have not taken 100-plus hours of accounting coursework or the CPA exam. As such, what follows are simply some thoughts and ideas about taxes and planning for them.

Taxes are a reality for every business owner, large and small, professional musicians included. Because we're on the topic of taxes, a "business-y" kind of thing, I'll dispense with the terms artist, musician, band, act, solo artist, and performer, as well as other musical monikers, and stick with "business owner," for the most part. It should help streamline things.

How business owners plan for taxes can mean the difference between starving and prospering or, worse, landing in front of a judge. Unfortunately, tax planning for many small business owners means little more than tossing receipts into a box and making an annual procession to a local strip mall retail tax preparer. You can do better—a lot better.

The tax code allows you to take advantage of various deductions. These deductions reduce your annual gross income, leaving you with your net annual income. This is the amount that is taxed. It sounds simple enough. Maximizing those deductions is a large part of tax planning and should be part of every business owner's financial strategy.

Many small business owners take steps to reduce their taxable income near the end of the year in a scramble to relieve their tax burden. Often, that's too late. Tax planning should be a year-round activity. Doing so will not only save you money in the not-too-long haul; it will also lower your anxiety level and make tax preparation a lot easier, so that April 15 is just another day.

For most businesses, the fiscal calendar is January through December. A fiscal calendar is the timeframe used for accounting income, expenses, and all that money stuff for a business. It can also be called a tax calendar. Although some businesses use different dates, for our purposes the standard calendar will do the trick, because it's easier to use as an example.

Now it's time to complicate matters a little. There are two ways of accounting for income and expenses—the cash method and the accrual method. The cash method is simple and straightforward. You account for income and expenses when you get the money or pay a bill—easy. It's the accounting method of choice for the majority of those operating as sole proprietors. Accrual is slightly more complex, and corporate entities must opt for it. With accrual, income is accounted for when a business has the right to receive it—in other words, usually when it's billed. Expenses are treated in a similar fashion and accounted for when a bill is due, rather than paid. The idea is to fairly accurately present a business's financial position during a particular accounting period. For many small business operations, such as bands, it's usually overkill, but for corporations and big-name acts with complex financial transactions, it makes a lot of sense. Actually, most big-name performers are corporations. Discuss your accounting method with your accountant, and be sure he or she explains the positives and negatives of each option for your business.

OBTAINING AN EMPLOYER IDENTIFICATION NUMBER (EIN)

U.S. citizens have Social Security numbers (SSNs) that are used to identify them for tax purposes and a variety of other matters. Businesses have employer identification numbers (EINs). EINs are used by employers, sole proprietors, corporations, partnerships, nonprofit associations, trusts, estates of decedents, government agencies, certain individuals, and other business entities. Think of it as an SSN for your business.

Applying for an EIN is easy and free. It can be done several ways, but the online application is the preferred method. Visit www.irs.gov for more information and to apply online. You can also download a PDF of Form SS-4 and complete the application by mail or fax. Application by phone is yet another option. Contact the toll-free business and specialty tax line at (800) 829-4933 between the hours of 7:00 AM and 10:00 PM Eastern Standard time, Monday through Friday. An assistor takes the information, assigns the EIN immediately, and provides the number to an authorized individual over the telephone.

PLANNING FOR INCOME TAXES

Businesses are responsible for filing income taxes on a quarterly basis, commonly called quarterlies. These are estimated tax liabilities and are usually based on the previous year's tax bill. Although paying taxes on a quarterly basis is more digestible for many small business owners, because it's a smaller amount than paying an entire year's worth of taxes, the IRS sees income tax payments for business as, more or less, a pay-as-you-go proposition. Quarterlies are not usually optional. Business owners are required to file quarterly if they expect to owe at least $1,000 in taxes for the current tax year, after subtracting any withholding and credits. They are also required to do this if the business expects withholding and credits to be less than the smaller of 90 percent of the tax to be shown on your current year's tax return, or 100 percent of the tax shown on your prior year's tax return. Get your estimates wrong and you will be penalized.

When using a standard January-to-December accounting calendar, taxes are due as follows: For the period of January 1 to March 31, taxes are due April 15; for April 1 to May 31, taxes are due June 15; for June 1 to August 31, taxes are due September 15; and finally, for September 1 to December 31, taxes are due January 15 of the following year. Failure to file quarterlies can also result in penalties.

Business owners can also make monthly estimated tax payments using the same tax form (1040-ES) as they would for quarterly payments. In addition, business owners can set up recurring monthly payments using the Electronic Federal Tax Payment System (EFTPS).

Depending on the state you live in, you may also need to make quarterly state income tax payments in addition to paying federal taxes. Also, be sure to check with your accountant, because there might be unique local tax laws that require additional payments.

TIPS FOR (RELATIVELY) PAINLESS TAXES

Relatively painless taxes might be an oxymoron. Nobody I know likes paying taxes every three months or more, and digging deep into one's pockets is not a pleasant experience. But, as mentioned, taxes are a reality of our business and personal lives. Here are a few thoughts about making the experience less painful.

Keep Excellent Records

If you plan to take a deduction, you'd better be sure you document it. The number-one reason the IRS will disallow a deduction is because there isn't an acceptable record to back it up. If the tedious task of recordkeeping isn't your cup of Earl Grey, you might consider using the services of a freelance bookkeeper or getting up to speed on using QuickBooks or other accounting software. If you keep your own books, you should set aside a specific time to record your transactions. Ideally, this would be daily or at least weekly. Doing it on a monthly basis or, worse, annually, can be a sure recipe for missing things, losing documents, and resorting to relying on memory. The IRS isn't fond of business owners' memories.

QuickBooks Pro, MYOB, Freshbooks, and other accounting software make it easy to keep track of your business's income and expenses. From that data the software will generate reports for your accountant, pretty much at the push of a button. Handy.

QuickBooks is a small business staple that has preset business categories and guides you through the initial setup process. It automatically sets up various income and expense categories that can be customized for your specific needs. Once it's set up, you simply enter the item, assign it to a category, and you're done. Financial reports can be generated that make your taxes and planning more accurate and easier. You might consider aligning your categories with those on the Schedule C. Doing so can save you and your tax preparer time when completing your tax returns.

Beyond this, you'll need a system to file receipts, invoices, and other documentation. Make copies and place one set in various folders designated for live performances; income sources, such as royalties, merchandise, and individual clients; equipment purchases; and vehicle-related expenses, repairs, and so on, while filing the originals in Annual Income and Annual Expenses folders. These can be further divided into various income and expense categories or subfolders or dividers. Accordion-type folders are good for this and are readily found at any office supply store. The idea here is to have everything in one accessible place. One set of folders is for income and expenses by source, while the other is a general set of files for income and expenses that will go to your accountant. If your accountant needs more specific information, it's easy to pull a particular income or expense folder and grab the information.

It's obvious that you'll want to keep receipts for all major business and project expenses. Paying $1,500 for a piece of sound equipment or $2,000 for vehicle repairs are expenses you're sure to want to keep track of. Likewise, spending several thousand dollars for a faster computer is an investment that should be documented and stored. But it's the smaller items that can be lost in the shuffle. They add up, and over the course of a year can prove to be a significant deduction. Office supplies are notorious for this. Or consider the musician who takes a quick trip out to the music store to pick up a couple of sets of strings, some nifty picks, and maybe an amp cord or three (not everybody's wireless, you know). The musician arrives back home to a ringing phone. The sales receipt gets lost in the shuffle and is never entered in the expenses record. Several small incidents like this over the course of a year can mean money is leaking out of the band's business.

Travel and Transportation

Travel and transportation can be significant for touring artists, but they are different things when it comes to accounting and taxes. Travel is going somewhere other than your business location for business reasons. Those reasons can include a performance, recording session, business meeting, or, perhaps, a conference. Transportation is how you get there, for example, driving, flying, or taking a train. The IRS defines travel as occurring when

- Your duties require you to be away from the general area of your tax home substantially longer than an ordinary day's work.

- You need to sleep or rest to meet the demands of your work while away from home.

Your tax home is defined as your regular place of business, regardless of where you maintain your family home. It includes the entire city or general area in which your business is located.

Qualified travel expenses can include airline tickets, hotel stays, meals, reasonable tips, ground transportation such as taxis or rental cars, fuel, tolls, and other business travel expenses. They include expenses incurred on the departure and return days, holidays, and layovers between business days that can't be avoided.

Transportation expenses are typically those travel-related expenses that are incurred during your regular day-to-day operations from your office, usually a home office for most musicians. For most people, transportation expenses will center around their vehicles. For city dwellers, they may also include subway fees, taxis, or bus fares. It's important to note that commuting costs are not deductible.

Vehicle expenses can be handled in a few ways. The IRS publishes a standard mileage rate. At the time of this writing in 2012, it's $0.55 per mile. To use this method, you must keep a record of miles driven specifically for business. If you choose the standard mile rate, you must use it for the first year the vehicle is available for business use. In subsequent years, you can change to actual expenses, if desired. For leased vehicles, if the standard rate is chosen, it must be used for the entire lease period.

Accounting for actual vehicle expenses is an alternative to using the standard mileage rate. It's more complex and requires more record-keeping, but it may be a better alternative, depending on your situation. Actual vehicle expenses include depreciation, lease payments, registration fees, licenses, gas, oil, insurance, repairs, tires, tolls, parking fees, and garage rent.

Finally, if your vehicle is used for both business and personal transportation, you must record how much mileage or actual expenses went toward business/band/music use.

For detailed information about travel and transportation deductions, download a free copy of IRS Publication 463, "Travel, Entertainment, Gift, and Car Expenses" at www.irs.gov.

Depreciation

Mention the word depreciation to most musicians, and you can see their eyes begin to glaze over. But in its basic form, it's not that tough of a concept. Although your accountant will make recommendations about depreciation, it's good to at least have a working knowledge of the concept. Also, having an understanding of depreciation helps a business owner plan larger purchases so that the timing provides the best tax advantage.

Let's start with a definition. *Depreciation* is defined as a portion of the cost that reflects the use of a fixed asset—a practice amp, for example—during an accounting period. Fixed assets are defined as business items that have useful lives of more than one year. An accounting period can be a month, a quarter, six months, or a full year.

Continuing with the amp example, let's say your need to sonically shatter the walls has aligned with a client's booking you for the biggest venue you've ever played, and you decide to invest in a top-end amp set-up that's going to set you back $8,000 when all is said and done. From an accounting point of view, let's say the useful life for this monster is five years. Using a one-year accounting period and the straight-line method of depreciation, the amount of depreciation is one-fifth, or $1,600. Eight thousand divided by five. That's easy enough to understand.

Moving on, things begin to get a bit more complex. There are two types of useful life durations for business assets. The first is used for book depreciation, which is used in accrual accounting. The second is used for tax depreciation. Because most artists will be using cash accounting, I'll address the latter. The IRS publishes a hefty, 120-page document titled "How to Depreciate Property." It's also called Publication 946 and is available for download at www.irs.gov. In it, the IRS provides a table listing various business fixed assets and the useful life for each.

Next is the method of depreciation. There are two primary ones. The first is straight line, which is the method used in the example above. Straight line is straightforward. Divide the cost of an item by its useful life. The second is accelerated depreciation, the most popular form of which is called double-declining balance. This method is based in the idea that an asset will get more use in its early years, thus justifying a higher depreciation amount in the earlier years.

Some items may be able to deduct the entire cost of an asset in the tax year it was purchased under Section 179 of the tax code. This is not depreciation, however. It's a deduction. There are some restrictions, so check with your accountant. For example, it's no surprise that the amount you deduct cannot be greater than your taxable income.

Home Office Deduction

The home office deduction is something of a double-edged sword. On one hand, you can deduct a portion of your personal expenses as business expenses. On the other hand, it can throw up a red flag to the IRS. Also, you can't take advantage of the home office deduction if you operated at a loss for the tax year. Obviously, you can't use the home office deduction to create a loss. The most you can use it for is reducing your profit to zero.

There are two methods to calculate the percentage used for your deduction. The first is by square feet. The second is by the number of rooms. To use square feet, measure your office space and then measure your home. The ratio of the two is the percentage you'll use to calculate your deduction. For example, let's say your office space is 150 square feet and your full house is 1,500 square feet. The ratio is 1:10 or 10 percent. Using the room method, divide one by the number of rooms. For example, if you have six rooms and use one for your office, your percentage would be 16 percent.

Other Deductions

Being a professional musician brings with it many potential ways to reduce your taxable income beyond the obvious deductions. To take advantage of the various possible deductions, they need to be documented. Be sure to save your receipts.

As a self-employed professional, you may be eligible to deduct your health insurance premiums and healthcare costs for you, your spouse, and dependents. If so, this can represent a significant reduction to your taxable income. The downside is that you can't deduct healthcare costs if you show a loss for the year. However, you can claim these costs on your personal Schedule A. Also, you cannot deduct any insurance costs for any months you were eligible to participate in a group health insurance plan through your or your spouse's employer.

If you're like me and use PayPal for billing, you can deduct the site's fees. Like other small businesses who are able to deduct credit card convenience fees, PayPal fees are a cost of doing business. PayPal makes it fairly easy, too. At the end of the year, simply print out your account activity. Strike any personal transactions and take the viable business expenses to your accountant.

While you can't deduct your primary home phone line, you can deduct a secondary line you use for business. If you use your mobile phone primarily for business, that can be a deductible expense, as well as Internet phone applications such as Skype, if you buy a phone number, voicemail, and other services.

Are you a member of any music union, associations, societies, or business- or music-related groups? Dues and membership fees are deductible. The same goes for educational expenses, trade publication subscriptions, business-related books, and fees paid to your attorney, accountant, and other professionals.

At one point or another in your business, a client's not going to pay you for services rendered or royalties due to you. Hopefully, this won't happen too often, but when it does, the amount should be deductible as a bad debt. Bad debts become deductible when the debt becomes totally worthless and uncollectible. There may be instances when a debt is partially worthless, but usually businesses wait until it's clear that the debt is completely worthless before taking the deduction.

How do you know if a debt is worthless? The best way is when the client informs you in no uncertain terms that he or she can't pay you. However, if there are good signs that a debt is worthless and you can back up this claim with facts, the debt can likely be deducted—for example, when the client has filed bankruptcy and there are miles of creditors in front of your claim. Another example would be when you haven't been paid after several months, and you learn that your client's phone is disconnected and the person is nowhere to be found.

SELF-EMPLOYMENT TAX

Being self-employed means being special. To the IRS, being "special" means having to pay your very own tax. It's how we pay into Social Security and Medicare. Unlike our payroll counterparts, who split these costs with their employers, we cover the full amount. The self-employment tax in 2010 is 13.3 percent, up to $106,800 of all net self-employment income. Above that amount, only the Medicare portion is paid. The Social Security portion is currently 10.4 percent, and Medicare is 2.9 percent.

There are times when an artist might want to contribute more than is required. For example, when the artist has had a bad year and takes a loss. The artist can opt to pay more in order to maintain or build up Social Security credits. Doing so requires using the aptly titled Optional Method. More information can be found within the Schedule SE instructions, available at www.irs.gov for the current tax year.

The only way to reduce this tax is to reduce taxable income. Regular deductions such as the standard deduction won't reduce this tax, and neither will health insurance costs nor individual 401(k) or SEP-IRA contribution deductions. Fortunately, half of the self-employment tax can be deducted, thus helping to reduce taxable income.

SALES TAXES

The sales tax question is something like herding cats or pushing a rope. In the United States, each state has its own sales tax requirements, so you should contact your state's sale tax department and certainly consult with your accountant. According to the National Retail Federation, forty-five states and 7,500 cities, counties, and jurisdictions impose sales taxes. Paying your accountant's fees is starting to sound like a very good investment at this point. An accountant's advice and recommendations can save you lots of headaches when you sell CDs, merchandise, and other products.

You have the ancient Egyptians to thank for all this. They imposed the first recorded sales tax on oil. The Greeks thought it was a great idea and also started doing it. But it was the Romans who spread the practice throughout Europe.

If you happen to be in a position where you must charge sales tax, you'll more than likely need to obtain a license. When you do that, you become an official tax collector with no direct benefit to your business. Such is the life of the small business owner. Nonetheless, collect you must. Be sure to review all your sales tax questions and concerns with your accountant. I can't stress that enough. You don't want the taxman knocking at your door.

You'll need a system in place to keep track of the tax money you've collected, prepare a return, and then send off the return, along with a check for the money collected, to the proper agency. Depending on the amount of taxes you collect, you can find yourself, or an outsourced service, working on sales taxes monthly, quarterly, or annually.

When it comes to sales taxes for merchandise and music sold online, the best thing to do is ask your accountant for guidance. Online sales tax can quickly become a can of worms, so it's best to ask the pro, who's much more up-to-date on online sales tax issues than you.

14

Pro Advice on How to Succeed

Here's a news flash: If the music business were easy, everybody would be a rock star or the next pop sensation. It's never been easy to get signed, write and perform a massive hit, and buy mansions, cars, and the accessories that go with being a star. Yet as you read this book, my hope is that you've found that musicians no longer need to play by the old rules. Sure, the competition is as fierce as ever—probably even more so than ever before. But, thanks to technological advances and a traditional music business that's in chaos, there are many opportunities to find success doing what you love.

The Future of Music Coalition is a nonprofit group that advocates for musicians. The Coalition began to conduct a survey in 2010 to learn about how musicians are generating revenue. The ongoing study has, so far, found forty-two different revenue sources.[24] That's more than incredible. No doubt, the musical landscape will continue changing and evolving.

The Internet has changed the distribution model and more. For example, the study referenced above found that 56 percent of respondents felt that the Internet made it possible for them to manage their own career, while 64 percent said that the Internet also made the music world more competitive by creating a massive quantity of music for consumer consumption. On a somewhat sadder note, 37 percent of the musicians surveyed said that they were spending more time on promotion and less time making music. You can find the survey (if still open) at futureofmusic.org/article/research/artist-revenue-streams.

The real burning question, which wasn't answered by the Coalition's survey, is whether or not artists are better off today, even though there's usually a lot more work involved beyond creating music. Or was the predictable path established long ago by the music industry a better way because of its predictability? That's a question each musician must answer for himself or herself. I suppose there are no right or wrong answers. It depends on a solo artist's or band's personal definition of success, their goals, and their drive. It rings back to the Tubes: "What do you want from life?"

ADVICE FROM THE TRENCHES

During the course of writing this book, I had the opportunity to interview several working professional musicians. Some are in bands. Others are solo acts. They run the gamut of musical genres. Here are some of the thoughts and advice they shared about starting and developing a career in music:

> I would say learning as much of the business end of things as possible. You are ultimately building a brand, your brand. I would get educated in both the music and music business sides of the industry. Whether you want to be a studio musician or songwriter for other musicians or just become a hired gun. Read every book possible about the subject, but don't get just book smart; get street smart. And what I mean by that is there is no better way to get out there and do the things that you need to do by just doing them in a real-world setting, your world.
>
> That's how I learned every aspect of the music industry—by wearing those different hats. I didn't have the luxury of having a major record label marketing department coordinating my mar-

keting plan for my release; that was me. I also did not have the luxury of hiring a top publicist to generate press about my music and my story; that was also me. Do you see the ongoing theme here?

This is a new era for the musician; it is no longer about just playing music and putting the blinders on to every other aspect of your career. The old music business model is dead! The playing field has definitely been leveled, which has made it even easier for artists and bands to get the word out on their music, but it has also made it harder to succeed because of the glut of people claiming to be musicians. It has become a double-edged sword.

Develop a thick skin because hearing the word "no" will become a large part of your lexicon when entering into the world of the music industry.

Ultimately, without great songs, you have nothing. If you believe you do and [believe] in yourself, then go for it; don't let anyone else tell you different!

Education and an undying belief in you[rself] would be my mantra!

Eric Knight, solo artist, singer/songwriter
www.ericknightonline.com

Don't wait for anyone or anything. Join professional groups, BMI, ASCAP, NARAS, NSAI, etc. Go to conferences. Never stop learning. Show up, pay attention, and keep a positive attitude. Think bigger.

Jim Popik, Ten Foot Tall
www.tenfoottallband.com

Seek God; stay clean; be diligent; be authentic; be true to yourself; find your voice; create your own signature.

Emilio Castillo, Tower of Power
www.towerofpower.com

I guess my advice would be to learn your instrument well, and to upgrade your recording and production skills. Most of all, I would advise artists to learn to write good songs—the sooner the better, either alone or with others—because even though the music business has changed in delivery over the years, it is still the business of songs that people enjoy, and singles are still the way to break new artists and keep existing artists in the public ear. Song revenue and covers of your songs on compilation albums and jingles/movie soundtracks (synch) can keep you in comfort for the rest of your life long after the bands you form split up and record sales decline.

This is why it's important to study or take a course in music business, to learn about the importance of copyright and revenue streams.

Rod Coombes, Stealers Wheel/Strawbs
www.stealerswheelofficial.com (soon to be launched)

Welcome to the team!

Things to remember: your love of music, the importance of thanking your opener and your headliner at shows, stylistic experimentation and growth, future-looking business savvy, the power of giving back to your fans, your true and real need for help (monetary and otherwise), and that professionalism is requisite; don't stoop.

Things to forget: bad shows, losing money on albums, bitterness, un-won contests, exclusion from "it" musician clubs, lousy press, no press, nay-sayers.

Emily Hurd, solo artist
www.emilyhurd.com

I would tell up-and-coming artists to be students of the game. Learn all you can and put 100 percent into it. Lastly, take advantage of technology; be open to starting and operating your own label so you can maintain ownership of your music and creativity.

Sean XLG, solo artist
www.seanxlg.com

The most important piece of advice I can give to any aspiring artist is to always *love* what you are doing. If you are feeling happy about the decisions you are making, then you are doing the right thing. The next *most* important thing to do is *build your connections.* Reach out to other professional musicians, producers, composers, vocalists, etc., and ask them about their experiences and point of views. You will learn a lot. This business is definitely built on relationships, so create them, nurture [them], and respect them. They will always give you the advantage.

Anna Fermin, singer/songwriter
www.annafermin.com

Take a cold, hard look at yourself and your services on a regular basis. Constantly ask yourself how you can improve and be even better.

Decide the one or two areas of your expertise and then pursue them in earnest. You can still diversify, but I think it's important to be an expert in at least one area.

Pigeonhole yourself before others do it for you. Others and your colleagues will forever describe you and your talents in a sentence or two. Decide what you'd want that sentence to say, write it down, and then use it to describe your services in perpetuity. Here is mine: "I'm an expert rock drummer that makes every song sound and feel great." (Wow—that should be my elevator pitch, too!)

Relationships are everything, so carefully nurture them and be grateful.

Be really good at what you do. If you're not, then do something about it.

Identify your potential client base. How will you get hired? Create an action plan. If it fails, make adjustments. You'll learn as you go.

Financial realizations and implications:

News flash—traditionally, musicians don't earn the lion's share of money in the biz. Managers, lawyers, promoters, and the like do. Get used to it.

The music business is rife with trust fund babies, people with "means," and musicians with "supportive" spouses. How will this affect you if you need to earn money for rent and groceries and they don't?

Image and perception are everything. Together, these will build your reputation. Then, your reputation will precede you wherever you go and whatever you do.

In public, act like a musician. In private, act like a businessperson. Do not let your private business persona overshadow the musician. In other words, don't air your number-crunching or bottom-line needs to a client or colleague. The music business is based on [being] hip and cool. It doesn't respond well to financial desperation or a "pay now" attitude. If, after tactful negotiation, the pay for this gig doesn't add up and make sense for you, politely tell them you're "not available" and would love to be considered in the future.

One last thing . . . there is no protocol or certification needed to enter the music business. Because of this, it's filled with all walks of life, from wackos to prodigies. It's also crammed with part-timers like your plumber and landscaper who can't wait to perform with their band *for free.*

Brian Doherty, solo artist
www.briandoherty.net

First of all, figure out what you do well and what your goals are. You may think you are good at your instrument, but if you want to make a living at this, you need to honestly assess your skills. This could mean going to school for music, auditioning for a band or orchestra, [or] going to jam sessions—getting into the environment where the best musicians play. I've met many people who think they can have a career as a musician but have little or no talent. Their teachers continue to take their money and feed their delusions, which does these people a great disservice. You have to be honest with people. That being said, I don't want to discourage people from following their passion.

You have to find your niche. If your goal is to land a job in an orchestra, you have to have a mastery of your instrument, [have] classical training, and know the repertoire inside and out. There is no way around this. If your goal is to make it as a punk rocker, it's more about attitude than technique, and you have to develop your skills as a songwriter, develop your stage presence, be on the scene, etc. Maybe you'll find that your passion for music will take you into the business end, managing or promoting artists, etc. Know what you want to do and what skill set it requires. Work to improve your weaknesses, and go for it.

I think the following guidelines apply if you want to have a successful career as a musician:

- Don't suck.

    Make sure you absolutely kick butt at what you do, whether it's singing or playing an instrument.
- Show up.

    In the words of legendary jazz bassist Charles Mingus, "Be on the scene." My good friend, guitarist Tony Pulizzi, took a big chance and moved his whole family to L.A. with no job prospects. He was pounding the pavement every night, going to every jam session he could find, making sure he was heard as much as possible, just being physically present on a regular basis. When you don't have a gig, your regular job should be looking for a gig. He did this persistently for two years before becoming the guitarist on *American Idol*. It also helps that he's an amazing musician.

• Honor the music.

Unless you already are a hugely successful musician and can get away with saying whatever you want, artists who are overly opinionated and refuse to open themselves to new styles and ideas rarely make it, and are usually pretty boring musicians. Be open to new influences. The more diversified you are, the more employable you'll be. I work a lot because I can play swing, metal, classical, bluegrass, [and] hip-hop. Those who specialize in one genre and put all their eggs in one basket [and] manage to make a living are a small minority.

• Have a good attitude and make the best of every situation.

Even if you are doing a crappy wedding gig with a bandleader who is a schmuck, playing music you don't care for, be professional and play it like it's the greatest piece of music ever written. No matter what you do, try to have fun and respect the people you are working with. If you're not having fun, you are wasting your time and everyone else's. Always put out positive energy, and it will be returned to you tenfold!

Joe Deninzon, Stratospheerius
www.stratospheerius.com
www.joedeninzon.com

Never forget: It is called playing music and not forcing music. So enjoy what you do!
Florian Opahle, Ian Anderson Touring Band
www.Florian-Opahle.com
www.j-tull.com

It's a tough business with a huge competition. Make yourself stand out, be original, push the boundaries of expectations, surprise, and, above all, think of how you can *give* instead of what you will *get*.

Also—don't expect everybody to like your music, and you won't be hurt when people don't. Bad criticism every now and then is unavoidable—try to not let it get a hold of you, brush it off, and focus on the people who do like your music.

Natalia "Saw Lady" Paruz, solo artist
www.SawLady.com

It's a lot of work. I spend far more time emailing, social networking, accounting, and driving than actually playing music. It requires luck, especially regarding whom you meet and what opportunities come your way. You have to be ready to work hard in order to take proper advantage of good opportunities.

Try to maintain as much financial independence and control as possible. We worked day jobs in order to finance our band, so that we could record and produce, and ultimately control and exploit, our first album.

It helps to have experience in other parts of the music business. Before starting JC Brooks & the Uptown Sound, I worked as a freelance music reviewer for TimeOut Chicago. That was incredibly helpful for several reasons.

Work to your strengths. If someone is organized and good with numbers, have them handle the money. If someone is bad at negotiating, don't have them book the gigs. Don't expect the introverts to be good at talking to people and selling stuff.

It helps to have an agreed-upon vision for the band, and the musical and stylistic choices should reinforce that vision, even at the expense of everyone's contributions having equal weight.

Be professional, punctual, polite, and prepared. People will want to work with you again if you aren't a pain in the ass to deal with.

Learn the sound guy's name, and tip him $20 at the end of the night if he made your life easier.

Ben Taylor, JC Brooks & the Uptown Sound
www.jcbrooksandtheuptownsound.com

As an artist in business for yourself, you have to develop a sense of separation between the business and creative standpoints. Develop a diligent team that have your best interest at heart, and believe 100 percent in what you are trying to obtain. Never act on impulse, and retrieve all the information before making a knowledgeable decision. Remember, it's your career; it's your vision. Be clear on what you want, [be] fearless in obtaining it, and always be fair.

Jullian James, solo artist
www.jullianjames.com

I have discovered, as an independent artist, that much of your time is spent hustling for gigs, updating social media, [and] promoting yourself and the band. That doesn't leave a lot of time for practice, and it can get *very* frustrating. Don't give up. You have got to learn to balance your life and use your time wisely.

Treat your body well. You can't keep up with the pace if you are overly tired, hungover, etc. Despite what people may believe, you *cannot* do your best work under the influence of anything. Stay focused . . . turn your body into a music *machine*!

You won't become the most popular band in town overnight, but the hard work is worth it in the end.

I am on the mailing list for DIY Musician. They have a lot of good information for independent artists, such as what makes a good webpage, how not to spam your fans, how to blog, importance of social media, etc. . . . just everything. I would recommend subscribing to this list. Great stuff.

Some of the best advice I have gotten: Work on your local following, create buzz, etc., and then work on your regional reputation. Keep building from there. It works! I began last year, creating a local following, and it has grown so much in a year. You are only as good as the *public* thinks you are.

We all have a lot more growing to do as musicians; however, if your audience thinks you're great, then other people will, too, even if they have never heard you. I get gigs from people who have heard of our reputation but have never actually heard us or seen us. Of course, once you get the gig, you'd better be able to prove you're worthy, but marketing is very important. Don't ignore that part.

I met someone in a music venue last weekend. When I was introduced, he said, "Wendy Hayes? I know you. I've heard your CD! You're awesome!" I was humbled and flattered. I never thought I would hear anything like that. I also felt suddenly shy and, at the same time, thrilled . . . thrilled because maybe, just maybe, all of this "stuff" I'm doing might just pay off in the end.

Wendy Hayes, Wendy Hayes Quartet
www.wendyhayes.net

Being a musician is labor intensive. You have to love doing it so much that the work involved feels worth it. You must practice and write, then get gigs and wrangle with idiots who fancy themselves as promoters—promoting is something they hardly ever do, so you promote—then get you and your band to the show. Do the show, [and] deal with sound guys who don't know what they are doing. When it's all over, you have to get paid, which sometimes involves threats and tactics [that are] less than ethical. Then you pack up all of your gear again, get in the tour vehicle, and head to the next gig for some more eye-opening abuse. Sometimes everything works out just right, but you can't get lazy. You must be ruthless in your persistence and keep your fans happy. It's all about the fans.

Lipbone Redding, Lipbone Redding & The LipBone Orchestra
www.lipbone.com

A LESSON FROM MICK JAGGER AND THE ROLLING STONES

Consider The Rolling Stones' front man, and rock icon, Mick Jagger. Jagger is no fool when it comes to making and investing money, maximizing opportunities, and keeping a watchful eye on the business bits. *Saturday Night Live* executive producer Lorne Michaels said of Jagger, "I think of him as coming from the English tradition of the actor-manager. If you watch him get ready to put on a show, you'll see that there is nothing that he is not aware of, that he is not intimately involved with, from lighting and design to how the curtain is going to hit the floor. There are very few people whose production skills impress me, but he's one of them. He's as good a showman and a producer as there is."[25]

Jagger's watchful eye helped make The Rolling Stones one of the richest bands in the history of rock and roll. In her *New York Times Style Magazine* article "Mick Without Moss," Zoe Heller wrote,

> When he is on the road, he has been known to keep a map in his dressing room, indicating the city at which the tour will go into profit. . . .
>
> The rise of illegal file sharing and the correspondingly steep worldwide decline in CD sales have made these tough times for record companies and recording artists alike. But the Rolling Stones continue to do very nicely, thank you. This is partly because what remains of the market for CDs is dominated by baby boomers—the Stones' demographic—and partly because Jagger, together with his recently retired financial adviser, Prince Rupert Loewenstein, has been exceptionally wily about exploiting other revenue streams. "There was a window in the 120 years of the record business where performers made loads and loads of money out of records," Jagger says. "But it was a very small window—say, 15 years between 1975 and 1990." Touring is now the most lucrative part of the band's business. (The Bigger Bang tour, from 2005 to 2007, raked in $558 million, making

it the highest-grossing tour of all time.) The band has also been ahead of the curve in recruiting sponsors, selling song rights and flogging merchandise. "The Stones carry no Woodstockesque, antibusiness baggage," Andy Serwer noted approvingly back in 2002 in *Fortune* magazine. Indeed. Their most recent merchandising innovations include a range of "as worn by" apparel, replicating garments that individual band members sported back in the '70s.[26]

Jagger and the Stones provide pointed lessons for the 21st-century artist. Not the least of these is to make great music and have loads of fun, but don't be ignorant or, worse, stupid when it comes to making, saving, and investing money. If you've taken my advice, you've put together a team of highly reliable, professional, and trustworthy advisors. Use them. Use them often. They can mean the difference between a comfortable career and retirement or one that's wrought with worry, uncertainty, and poverty.

There are those who will say Jagger and the Stones sold out along the way. Let them. They're entitled to their opinion. It seems Mick doesn't think so, nor does he appear to care if people think so. As for me, after almost fifty-seven years on this planet, I've learned that having some money in your pocket is loads better than being broke. Beyond that, people with talent and the smarts to leverage it are entitled to be compensated for their efforts.

FINDING YOUR POSITION IN YOUR FANS' HEADS

No matter what genre your music is, these days, artists, bands, and professional musicians must find their unique position in an overwhelming musical marketplace of songs and potential fans. It's important to be creative and maximize your talents. But it's also paramount to treat your act as the business it is in order to be successful. Maximize each and every opportunity to sell and license your music and merchandise. Most of all, gain a thorough understanding of your audience. Learn what's important to them and what they want. Then find ways to give it to them. Doing that simple task is another "make-it-or-break-it" piece of advice. Remember, without a solid fan base, you might have stellar music but little success, both creatively and financially. Sellout performances, record deals, through-the-roof merchandise sales, and so on are a result of your fans and what you bring to them.

If you can't write a description of your ideal fans on the back of a matchbook cover, you don't have a clear idea of who they are. Invite them to comment on Facebook, reply to tweets, email you, and such. It's all about interacting. With interaction comes understanding.

Find ways to interact with your fan base, both at live shows and offstage. Find ways to get a wee bit intimate (and I don't mean inviting them backstage after a show). I mean that inasmuch as you need to learn about them, they need to learn about you. Don't be afraid to reveal some of yourself. Why did you write this or that song? What do you and the band members do beyond playing and recording? What's important to you? All this makes you a little more human and less of a commodity that's bought, sold, and shared among friends. It will also help keep you grounded when things start getting slightly weird. Sure, you need to create and develop a brand, but you also need to stay human.

Be aggressive in growing your fan base and creating evangelists for your music and live shows. Evangelists, or, even better, "efangelists" (Cool! I'm creating my own language!), will do more for your career and musical expansion than anything else—even more than a record company, PR campaign, or Facebook. The word *fan* comes from the word *fanatic*. That's what you want to develop. A (large) group of fanatics for your music who tell everybody they meet about you, your shows, your CDs, your downloads, and your merchandise.

HONE YOUR BUSINESS SKILLS

Your fans are responsible for making you successful. You are responsible for maintaining and managing that success now and into the future. That takes business savvy. Your team of advisors, your manager, your agent, and your PR folks will help you out, but at the end of the day, the ultimate responsibility falls into your lap. It's your choice to meet it head on and grab it by the horns or let your career simply happen to you. Like Mick Jagger, know where the money's coming in and going out. Maximize the things that sell and dump the ones that don't and are probably costing you money.

Attend some of the numerous conferences, workshops, and similar events to learn better business skills and what's working and what's not. You will meet many like-minded souls with whom you can share war stories and experiences. Much of the music business is about connections, and these are the places to make some.

In the United States alone there are more than 100 conferences to choose from for artists and music industry folks. Some are ridiculously expensive, while others are more within the, shall we say, limited budget of the typical band or solo performer. Here are a few to check out. You can also find a listing of music conferences at www.musicnomad.com/ Support_Your_Music/Music_Industry_Conferences_Trade_Shows.

- CMJ Music Marathon and Film Festival, www.cmj.com/marathon/conference

    If you're into college music, both performing and radio, this might be a good event for you.
- ASCAP Expo, www.ascap.com

    A good one for meeting songwriters and attending mentoring sessions with seasoned pros.
- Billboard and The Hollywood Reporter Film and TV Music Conference,   www1.billboardevents.com/billboardevents/filmtv/

    This is a good one to meet musical directors. If you're looking to license your songs, this might be the place to make some connections.
- South by Southwest Music, sxsw.com

    This is a massive and extremely well-known conference for interactive products, film, and music with a twenty-five-year history. The music portion is six days. From the event website: "By day, thousands of conference registrants network in the halls of the Austin Convention Center on their way to do business in the SXSW Trade Show, sit in on informative panel discussions featuring some of the industry's key players, gain insight from legendary keynote speakers or plan out their abundant party schedules. At night, SXSW showcases roughly 2,000 musical acts from around the globe, representing well over 50 different countries, on over 90 stages in downtown Austin."

- Pollstar Live, www.pollstarpro.com

    This is a good place to meet venue promoters, get on a better tour, or meet managers of top acts.

Although conferences can be great places to meet people, make contacts, and attend a slew of sessions, workshops, panel discussions, and more, the registration fees are just the start. Don't forget you'll need to get there, which normally involves plane fare. You'll need to book a hotel, eat, and probably buy some stuff. But if you can afford it, go for it!

BALANCING YOUR PROFESSIONAL AND PERSONAL LIVES

It's said that all work and no play makes for a dull person. Music, although wonderful, can easily become an all-encompassing endeavor when you're a professional. We find ourselves working on music, looking for gigs, or both as the clock ticks on. We start our day early, and before we know it, it's 8:30 PM, 9:00 PM, or later as we tweak a lyric or wrestle with a melody that refuses to behave. We think, "I'll just finish this up on Saturday morning," and yet another weekend slips away with evening gigs, rehearsals, writing, business tasks, and more.

Although you love what you do and need to get the work done, it's important to your health and well-being to set up boundaries and stick to them. In keeping with your newfound business sense, open the door by working too late, on the weekends, or on holidays, and that door becomes awfully tough to close later on down the road.

Friends and family can also be taxing on a self-employed musician. They tend to think that just because you're a musician and don't have a "real" job, you're always available to run errands for them, pick up the kids, and do this or that. If you don't clearly communicate that you're working and that your musical career is just as important as their day jobs are, emotions can get the better of you, and anger can quickly set in.

We work to better our lives. Yet by overdoing it, our personal lives and relationships with family and friends suffer. We may have decided to be a professional musician as a way to gain more freedom in our lives, yet we end up achieving the exact opposite of what we set out to do and become a slave to our band and its business. When we work too much, we set ourselves up for exhaustion and burnout or drugs as a way to calm our head. If that happens, you won't be any good to your clients, family, and friends.

Think about why you do this work. What is your attitude toward your profession and your business? Are they a means toward an end, or do you see them as ends unto themselves? Many artists define themselves by their work. When that happens, they can have a difficult time separating themselves from their band business. They put themselves on the treadmill and believe they must work and work to feel good about themselves. It's a form of addiction that can be next to impossible to break. Plus, it can all too easily lead to more destructive addictions. Think of all the artists we've lost to drugs. They may still be heard on the radio or on CDs, but that talent is lost forever. No more new music . . . ever.

Taking personal time for hobbies, spending time with family and friends, or simply taking a walk can be energizing. A vacation to a new place can spark ideas and enhance your creativity. Speaking of vacation, it's a good idea to actually save for one and schedule it. A week or two away from performing and recording can give you entirely new insights into your music.

In the end, you are more than your music and its related work. You're more than a nice melody, a great beat, and harmonies. If you become overly absorbed in your work, you risk missing the life you were meant to live. I don't mean to offend those who are into reincarnation, but I believe we get only one shot at life. Strive to keep things in perspective. Work and your business are simply a means toward an end. That end should be having a complete, satisfying, and fulfilling life that's punctuated by music.

MONEY MANAGEMENT THOUGHTS

Richard J. Leider, author of *The Power of Purpose: Find Meaning, Live Longer, Better*, writes, "Time is the most precious currency of life, and how we spend it reflects what we truly value. Once an hour is gone, it is gone forever. It cannot be re-earned."[27] Money, on the other hand, can be re-earned, saved, and invested.

Money is a funny thing. All artists want it to buy things to help make better music, grow their fan base, and provide a level of comfort for themselves and their families. Yet many of us are afraid to talk about it. Thoughts such as "I stink at numbers," or "I'll just let the venue producer toss out a number first," pervade our minds and hinder us from being the best we can be. How we think about money is at the core of how well or how poorly we manage it.

My colleague and friend Ilise Benun of Marketing Mentor recently published her book *The Creative Professional's Guide To Money: How to Think About It. How to Talk About It. How to Manage It*. Although it's targeted to designers, writers, and visual creatives, the content is just as valuable to musicians. She was gracious enough to share a few thoughts on how we develop a relationship with money:

> When I think about how people think about money, it's in a larger context of how they think about their business. The first part of the book talks about how to adjust or evolve your mind-set into a business mind-set, which includes how you think about money, how you set goals, how you think about

your pricing, and how you position your pricing. All of these things are part of that process. . . .

When it comes to one's money mentality, and how it's set, I'm not a psychologist, but I do have a worksheet in the book called "What Are Your Money Issues?" that begins by looking at your history, because a lot of it does happen early on. I'm not exactly sure how the money mind-set gets formed, although I think it happens very early. It helps to figure out what those different experiences or memories are that may be getting in the way of treating your business like a business, especially when it comes to money. I do think that whatever it was, or however it started, it can definitely be changed."[28]

MONEY MANAGEMENT TIPS

Taking personal time for family vacations, going out to dinner or to the theater, and engaging in hobbies aren't likely to happen if you're strapped for cash. Even if you have good cash flow, money can easily and swiftly leak through your fingers if you're not careful. For example, you land a licensing deal and get a royalty check for $5,000. But you quickly spend it on things you *think* you need. Pretty soon, it's gone, and you really have no idea where it all went. Then the landlord comes, knocking on the door, wanting the rent. It happens all too often in the indie music world.

In *The Money Book for Freelancers, Part-Timers and the Self-Employed*, authors Joseph D'Agnese and Denise Kiernan write, "Having your financial house in order brings peace of mind. It also puts you in a better position to survive and thrive, no matter what the economic climate."[29]

In a similar vein, author Tom Robbins once said, "There's a certain Buddhistic calm that comes from having . . . money in the bank."[30]

It's true. When there's more month than money, anxiety rears its ugly head, and you can't do your best work when you're constantly worried about money. Plus, by not having a money management strategy in place, your finances can quickly turn into something that resembles a game of whack-a-mole gone horribly wrong. You find yourself worried, forever robbing Peter to pay Paul, never seeming to catch up.

Feast-or-famine syndrome is common plight for musicians without a money management plan. It's a roller coaster ride that can drive many full-time musicians back to the nine-to-five cubicle world. To avoid it, artists must always be aggressively marketing their act and putting money away for the all-too-common rainy day.

Separating your business money from your personal money is central to a money management strategy. You should have both a business checking account for your act or band and a personal checking account. Although artists working as sole proprietors technically take a draw from the business instead of an actual salary, consider drawing a set amount each week or every other week, if possible. It helps to make things much more predictable and makes it easier to manage your personal money.

When a gig deposit comes in, set it aside in a kind of escrow account and hold it until the show is completed. Sure, it can be a tough thing to do, but if you adequately capitalize your musical business at its startup, you won't need to completely rely on sporadic revenue to pay your personal and business bills. That usually means having at least three to four months' worth of working capital when you launch your full-time music career. Keeping these funds out of your daily finances also ensures that you'll have the money if something goes awry and you need to make a refund. It happens. A show gets cancelled for some reason. A music director suddenly turns into a nightmare, and you'd rather not work with that person. Of course, you could make your deposits nonrefundable, but that can turn clients away.

Taxes are another thing that will take a chunk of your check. Put aside roughly 30 percent to cover them, and pay income taxes on a quarterly basis. You'll also need to put money aside to cover your overhead expenses, equipment, repairs, marketing, insurance, and such. These can be separate bank accounts or just accounts within your accounting software. The trick is using this money as it was intended, and not on other things. It requires some self-discipline, but it's a habit that can be learned.

Noted designer and business mentor Peleg Top is a creative entrepreneur with more than twenty years of experience running his own design firm and mentoring creatives. He's also co-author of *The Designer's Guide to Marketing and Pricing.* In it, he shares his personal money management system. His system can easily be adapted for the musically inclined, especially solo acts. He recommends setting aside 30 percent of income for taxes to start. What's left will be considered 100 percent. From this, allocate 60 percent as a lifestyle account. These funds cover your house payment or rent, groceries, and other day-to-day necessities or your band members' cut. Ten percent is set aside as a wealth account for investments. Once the money goes into this account, never touch it again. Five percent goes to your joy account. This is money that funds the fun things in life, such as going out to dinner, catching a movie, and so on. Your dream account is used for bigger things, such as vacations, a new car, or a house; a nifty new Les Paul; ten percent is set aside for this purpose. Five percent goes to your enlightenment account and is used for things like personal or business growth, continuing education, training, or coaching. Finally, ten percent goes to a spiritual growth account and is used for tithing, donations, and so on.

Start saving and investing early—the earlier, the better. The longer you wait, the more difficult it is to achieve financial independence and have a comfortable retirement. Sure, for many readers, retirement is a long way off, but thinking and planning for it now will help ensure you're not greeting people at Wal-Mart when you're seventy-five.

Here's a reality check: The richest Americans are investors and savers. Of those who have an income of $1 million or more, only one-third of their income is generated from their job or business. The rest comes from investments. Getting your piece of the pie means investing and saving.

Investing works over time due to the miracle of compound interest. It makes your savings and investment grow almost exponentially. In his book *Become a Recognized Authority in Your Field in Sixty Days or Less,*

Bob Bly writes, "If you were to open an IRA at age 50, and contribute $2,000 a year earning 8 percent compounded monthly, at age sixty-five your IRA would be worth $54,300. Had you opened the same IRA when you were twenty-five, and put in the same amount of money annually earning the same rate of return, at age sixty-five your IRA would be worth more than half a million dollars—almost ten times as much."[31]

Consider finding a good financial planner to advise you as to the best strategy for your age. Be sure he or she is an authentic financial planner and not an insurance agent trying to sell you his company's insurance products. There are loads of them out there.

A little bit of something is a lot better than a whole lot of nothing. That certainly goes for saving, investing, and living. Find ways to cut costs, but make sure they make sense. By that I mean that sometimes it doesn't make economic sense to do something that appears to save you money but really doesn't. This is also called being penny wise and dollar foolish. For example, driving all around town to save a couple of cents on a gallon of gasoline probably doesn't make too much sense. You'd probably burn up more fuel looking for a bargain than you would have saved. Similarly, when it comes to band work, are you doing tasks that take away from your time doing things that generate income? You might be better off outsourcing them and focusing your efforts on revenue-generating activities, such as marketing and promotion and making industry contacts through phone calls, email, and personal meetings.

Here are words that should be etched in stone: Live below your means. That doesn't mean going without. It means being frugal. It's also worthwhile to note that most millionaires don't drive luxury cars or live in mansions. They're the couple next door, driving a ten-year-old car that they've taken care to maintain. That's why they're millionaires. They watch what they spend their money on, they save, and they invest.

In the United States, we live in a world of status symbols. Many people finance their lifestyle with credit cards in an effort to appear wealthier than they are, just to impress the folks next door. America has become a nation of high-volume consumers who must have the latest toy. As a matter of fact, CreditCard.com reports that the average credit card debt per household with this type of debt is a whopping $15,788.[32] Even scarier, 36 percent of respondents in a FINRA Investor Education Foundation survey said they didn't know the interest rate on the card they use most often.[33]

Case in point: When I started my business in the mid 1980s, I was young and stupid. I simply had to have an Acura with a car phone. This was well before mobile phones were commonplace. Granted, it was the best car I ever owned, and I bought out the lease early. But did I really need it? Probably not. In retrospect, I should have bought a pre-owned car and invested the rest of the money into my business. Alas, hindsight is twenty-twenty.

Before making a purchase, especially a major one, it's a good idea to wait about thirty days. Buying on impulse can be a major way for money to leak out of your musical business and your life. After a thirty-day cooling-off period, you may find the item isn't as needed or as important as you originally thought. If you still want it after thirty or so days, go ahead and buy it.

Living below your means and finding ways to be frugal will help ensure that you can meet your obligations each month and put some money away. A musical career can be somewhat up and down, especially in the beginning. Be sure you know your numbers. Those include how much you spend in your business and personal arenas each month, what you owe, what you own, and what you bring in on average each month. Taming your finances brings with it a lot of freedom.

PLAN FOR RETIREMENT OR DIE ONSTAGE . . . OR IN THE STUDIO

Oh sure, it might sound glorious to drop dead on stage, especially for the death metal crew. Here's a chilling, hardcore reality: If you don't plan for retirement, odds are you'll end up working until you depart this Earth. Being an eighty-five-year-old lead guitarist on oxygen isn't too glorious, either. Okay, Keith Richards exempted. And here's a not-so-fun factoid to go with it: According to Maiolo of IndyWeek.com, ". . . between 15 and 16 percent of Americans don't have health insurance, but 45 percent of musicians are uninsured. And out of the 55 percent of musicians that actually carry health insurance, only 5 percent have insurance because of their job in music. That 5 percent is largely comprised of orchestra members and session musicians, not your average touring rock 'n' roller. The remainder have health insurance through another job or because they pay out of pocket for an individual plan." Strikingly sad and scary.

You might be in your twenties or thirties right now, when retirement seems a lifetime away, but sixty-five will arrive quicker than you expect. Without a retirement plan and the savings to go with it, you'll still be working to make ends meet. But in your mid to late sixties, will you still be relevant and working in music? Will you even want to? Several big names, including McCartney, Jagger, and loads of others, do and continue to perform, write, and make loads of money. But they're the exception to the rule. The way things are going, it's a safe bet you won't be able to count on Social Security to keep you afloat. This can mean that without a substantial savings, you can easily find yourself bagging groceries to make ends meet. Sure, you'll be dining on salmon and tuna, but it will be from a can meant for your feline friend.

Is all this meant to scare the heck out of you? Absolutely!

Begin with a simple savings account. Get into the habit of saving a certain percentage of each check. It doesn't need to be a lot in the beginning. Five or even 10 percent will do. The point is to get you into the habit of saving. It will also help you build an initial minimum amount required by some retirement accounts.

There are a daunting number of investment vehicles available. Which one is right for your situation can be tough to sort out. Investing in the services of a financial planner can be wise. The planner will review your present situation, your age, and your goals. Then he or she will recommend the best type of account. Be sure to find an authentic financial planner. Some insurance agents will promote themselves as financial planners, but they will try to sell you their company's products, often annuities or other insurance products, which may not be the best choice for you. Ask around to get some referrals. When you find a few, be sure to ask them if they've worked with musicians. That's important, because a full-time, self-employed artist's needs are very different from those of the artist's nine-to-five counterparts.

Those counterparts have the benefit of pension plans, matched contributions to 401(k) plans, and profit sharing. A self-employed musician has none of these, and that means you'll need to put away more for that rainy day.

Finally, in addition to getting the advice of a financial planner, be sure to run your plan by your accountant. Your accountant can make suggestions and provide insights that may make your dream of retirement a faster reality.

A CLOSING WORD

Starting on the path to becoming a full-time career musician who is self-employed will bring with it many challenges but also many rewards. By taking the time to carefully plan your business just as much as, if not more than, your music and show and then implement that plan, you will set yourself apart from others who didn't take the time or do the homework.

As you build your career, aggressively market your act to create a pipeline of qualified contacts. Doing so will allow you the benefit of taking on only those gigs and projects that you enjoy and are a good fit for your business. Mind your credit and cash flow, and take care to manage your money. Strive to create music and exceed your fans' expectations at every step along the way. Do the same for all your industry contacts as well.

If you do these things, the bounty will be a lifestyle that brings you flexibility, steady income, and much less stress than your counterparts—

those who simply let their music business happen to them rather than taking responsibility and initiative.

Plan for your retirement early on, and work toward building a nest egg that will allow you to retire in comfort. If you do, you can look back and think, "What a rewarding ride it's been!"

Resources

BOOKS

- *Music Business Handbook and Career Guide*, by David Baskerville
- *Music, Money and Success*, by Jeffrey and Todd Brabec
- *The Business of Music: The Definitive Guide to the Music Industry*, by William Krasilovsky and Sidney Shemel
- *All You Need to Know About the Music Business*, by Donald Passman
- *A Music Business Primer*, by Diane Rapaport
- *What They'll Never Tell You About the Music Business: The Myths, the Secrets, the Lies (& a Few Truths)*, by Peter Thall

WEBSITES AND BLOGS FOR PROMOTION AND COMMUNITY

- iLike, www.iLike.com
- Last.fm, www.last.fm.com
- OurStage, www.ourstage.com
- MP3.com, www.mp3.com
- iTunes, www.iTunes.com
- MusicNomad, www.musicnomad.com
- Music Business Journal, mbj.berkleemusicblogs.com
- Digital Music News Blog, www.digitalmusicnews.com

- DIY Musician Blog from CD Baby, www.diymusician.cdbaby. com
- New Music Strategies, newmusicstrategies.com
- Music Think Tank, www.musicthinktank.com
- Bob Baker's Indie Music Promotion Blog, music-promotion-blog.blogspot.com

SOCIAL MEDIA COMMUNITIES AND TOOLS FOR MUSICIANS

- Facebook, www.facebook.com
- Twitter, www.twitter.com
- MySpace. www.myspace.com
- HootSuite, www.hootsuite.com
- Social Oomph, www.socialoomph.com
- TweetDeck, www.tweetdeck.com

ONLINE SERVICES FOR MUSICIANS

- ReverbNation, www.reverbnation.com
- SonicBids, www.sonicbids.com
- iTunes, www.iTunes.com
- JinglePunks, www.jinglepunks.com
- Indaba, IndabaMusic.com
- SoundCloud, soundcloud.com
- CDBaby, www.cdbaby.com
- About.com/Musicians, musicians.about.com/u/sty/companyprofiles/onlineservices/

CD DUPLICATION AND RELATED SERVICES

- Diskmakers, www.diskmakers.com
- MasterCopy, www.cdmastercopy.com

- DiskFaktory, www.diskfaktory.com
- BeyondConcepts, www.bcduplication.com

MERCHANDISE SUPPLIERS

- CaféPress, www.cafepress.com
- BandWear, bandwear.com
- Cooler Stubbies, www.coolerstubbies.com
- Blueberry Ink, www.blueberryink.com
- Identity Links, www.identity-links.com

EQUIPMENT AND INSTRUMENTS

- Guitar Center, www.guitarcenter.com
- Sam Ash, www.samash.com
- Musician's Friend, www.musiciansfriend.com
- Paradiddles Drum Shop, www.paradiddlesdrumshop.com

LEGAL SERVICES FOR MUSICIANS

- Music Law, www.music-law.com
- Music Legal Forms, www.musiclegalforms.com
- Nolo, www.nolo.com
- Free Advice (music law), www.freeadvice.com/law/

ASSORTED COLLECTION OF RESOURCES FOR MUSICIANS

- Neon Egypt, www.neonegypt.com/resources.htm

Notes

1   U.S. Bureau of Labor Statistics, "Musicians and Singers," www.bls.gov/ooh/
     entertainment-and-sports/musicians-and-singers.htm.

2   IMDb, "Briography for Jon Bon Jovi," www.imdb.com/name/nm0000954/
     bio.

3   Dr. John L. Vitale, "Formal and Informal Music Learning: Attitudes and
     Perspectives of Secondary School Non-Music Teachers," *International Journal
     of Humanities and Social Science* 5 (2011).

4   Wikipedia, "List of band name etymologies," http://en.wikipedia.org/wiki/
     List_of_band_name_etymologies.

5   Al Ries and Jack Trout, *Positioning: The Battle for Your Mind* (New York:
     McGraw Hill, 2000).

6   *Royal Pingdom*, "Internet 2011 in numbers," royal.pingdom.
     com/2012/01/17/internet-2011-in-numbers/.

7   Email Marketing Reports, "Why do email marketing?," www.email-mar-
     keting-reports.com/basics/why.htm.

8   gaebler.com, "Typical Direct Mail Response Rates," www.gaebler.com/
     Direct-Mail-Response-Rates.htm.

9   http://www.HowManyAreThere.org.

10   intomobile, "Analysts say that by 2016 you'll stream all your music [Some of
     us are already there]," http://www.intomobile.com/2011/03/24/analysts-
     say-2016-youll-stream-all-your-music-some-us-already-there/.

11   ABIresearch, "Mobile Cloud Music Services," http://www.abiresearch.
     com/research/product/1006442-mobile-cloud-music-services/.

12   *Chicas Productions*, "Cloud-Based Music Streaming Will Be Dominant by
     2016 (Study)," http://chicas-productions.blogspot.com/2011/03/cloud-
     based-music-streaming-will-be.html.

13   Dan Reitz Dot Com, "Spotify? Not much better than piracy. Sorry," http://
     danreitz.com/blog-spotify-piracy/.

14   David Ogilvy, *The Unpublished David Ogilvy* (London: Profile Books, 2012).

15   Kenny Love, Ezine articles, "College Radio: The Most Important Radio
     Level for Musicians," http://ezinearticles.com/?College-Radio:-The-Most-
     Important-Radio-Level-for-Musicians&id=39271.

16   Ibid.

17   Jason Ankeny, all music, "Joni Mitchell," www.allmusic.com/artist/joni-mitchell-mn0000270491.

18   recmusicbeatles.com, "Re: Searching for Yesterday," www.recmusicbeatles.com/public/files/saki/yesterday-saki.html.

19   Moses Avalon.com, "Why You Should Think Twice . . . ," http://www.mosesavalon.com/why-you-should-think-twice-before-joining-ascap-bmi-or-sesac-part-ii-non-profit-nonsense/.

20   Renee C. Quinn, IPWatchdog, "Michael Jackson and the Beatles Copyrights," http://www.ipwatchdog.com/2009/07/01/michael-jackson-and-the-beatles-copyrights/id=4363/.

21   Wikipedia, "Copyright Act of 1976," en.wikipedia.org/wiki/Copyright_Act_of_1976.

22   Wikipedia, "Work for hire," en.wikipedia.org/wiki/Work_for_hire.

23   Mike King, *Music Business and Trend Monitoring*, "Blue Note: The Best Music Discovery App on Spotify," http://mikeking.berkleemusicblogs.com/?s=The+overall+theme+of+the+panels+I+attended+this+year#.

24   Future of Music Coalition, "Artist Revenue Streams," http://futureofmusic.org/article/research/artist-revenue-streams.

25   Zoe Heller, The New York Times Style Magazine, "Mick Without Moss," http://www.nytimes.com/2010/12/05/t-magazine/5well-mick-dek.html?pagewanted=all&_r=0.

26   Ibid.

27   Richard J. Leider, *The Power of Purpose: Find Meaning, Live Longer, Better* (San Francisco: Berrett-Koehler Publishers, 2010).

28   Ilise Benun, *The Creative Professional's Guide To Money: How to Think About It. How to Talk About It. How to Manage It* (Cincinnati: HOW Books, 2011).

29   Jospeh D'Agnese and Denise Kiernan, *The Money Book for Freelancers, Part-Timers and the Self-Employed* (New York: Three Rivers Press, 2010).

30   Always Frugal, "Quotations about Saving Money," http://www.alwaysfrugal.com/saving-money.html.

31   Robert W. Bly, *Become A Recognized Authority In Your Field - In 60 Days Or Less* (New York: Alpha Books, 2001).

32   Ben Woolsey and Matt Schulz, creditcards.com, "credit card statistics. industry facts, sebt statistics," http://www.creditcards.com/credit-card-news/credit-card-industry-facts-personal-debt-statistics-1276.php.

33   FINRA Investor Education Foundation, *Financial Capability in the United States* (Washington D.C.: FINRA Investor Education Foundation, 2009).

Index

Books from Allworth Press

Allworth Press is an imprint of Skyhorse Publishing, Inc. Selected titles are listed below.

Making and Marketing Music: The Musician's Guide to Financing, Distributing, and Promoting Albums
by Jodi Summers (paperback, 6 x 9, 240 pages, $18.95)

Making It in the Music Business: The Business and Legal Guide for Songwriters and Performers, Revised Edition
by Lee Wilson (paperback, 6 x 9, 288 pages, $18.95)

Rock Star 101: A Rock Star's Guide to Survival and Success in the Music Business
by Marc Ferrari (paperback, 5 1/2 x 8 1/2, 176 pages, $14.95)

How to Grow as a Musician: What All Musicians Must Know to Succeed
by Sheila Anderson (paperback, 6 x 9, 256 pages, $22.95)

Gigging: A Practical Guide for Musicians
by Patricia Shih (paperback, 6 x 9, 256 pages, $19.95)

Booking and Tour Management for the Performing Arts, Revised Edition
by Rena Shagan (paperback, 6 x 9, 288 pages, $19.95)

The Diva Next Door: How to Be a Singing Star Wherever You Are
by Jill Switzer (paperback, 5 ½ x 8 ½, 208 pages, $19.95)

The Songwriter's and Musician's Guide to Nashville, Revised Edition
by Sherry Bond (paperback, 6 x 9, 256 pages, $18.95)

Career Solutions for Creative People
by Dr. Ronda Ormont (paperback, 320 pages, 6 x 9, $19.95)

The Quotable Musician: From Bach to Tupac
by Sheila E. Anderson (hardcover, 7½ x 7½, 224 pages, $19.95)

Creative Careers in Music
by Josquin des Pres and Mark Landsman (paperback, 6 x 9, 224 pages, $18.95)

The Art of Writing Great Lyrics
by Pamela Philips Oland (paperback, 6 x 9, 272 pages, $18.95)

How to Pitch and Promote Your Songs, Third Edition,
by Fred Koller (paperback, 6 x 9, 208 pages, $19.95)

The Secrets of Songwriting: Leading Songwriters Reveal How to Find Inspiration and Success
by Susan Tucker (paperback, 6 x 9, 256 pages, $19.95)

To see our complete catalog or to order online, please visit *www.allworth.com*.